The Lie Detection Manual v2.0
Becoming a Human Lie Detector

WARNING

Once you read this book,
You will look at the world
In a different light.

ISBN 1-4116-1821-1

Web site: www.Net4TruthUSA.com
Bookstore: www.LuLu.com/Net4TruthUSA

COPYRIGHT NOTICE

THE LIE DETECTION MANUAL v2.0
Becoming a Human Lie Detector

© Copyright 2004, 2006 - David Todeschini - all rights reserved
Web site: http://www.Net4TruthUSA.comm E-mail: dave44mag4u@aol.com

" You can fool some of the people all the time, and those are the ones you need to concentrate on". [1]

– George W. Bush

NOTE: For the sake of clarity and expediency, words that are not likely to be in the public's vocabulary, words that are commonly misunderstood, or those that are used differently than their common use in this text, are tagged with footnote numbers the first time they are encountered in the text.

PLEASE: Never go past a word that you do not understand. I have footnoted all of the words that are likely to be misunderstood. The footnotes are located at the bottom of each page.

This book is meant to be read in sequence; prior concepts are required in order to adequately comprehend what follows in the text. You will get more out of your reading experience if you take your time, and read carefully, following all of the footnotes for definitions of words.

IMPORTANT: If you are viewing this as an "electronic document" or as an "E-book", or web page, clicking on the underlined links such as: www.Net4TruthUSA.com will automatically start your web browser (if it is not already running). This will connect you to the Internet, and take you to the referenced web site.

Author's Note: I urge you to follow the links and footnotes in this book. Much valuable information can be obtained pertaining to your particular application of the technology described herein, if you utilize the resources that have been made available. Please also visit my web site at www.Net4TruthUSA.com often, as I will be constantly updating it.

---

[1] Source: Gannett NEWS Service - USA Today, August 14, 2003 article by James Bovard.

INTRODUCTION

By: David Todeschini

This book is NOT a manual on how to operate a Polygraph[2] machine… at least not the type of "Lie Detector" that you plug into the wall and hook up to a person with wires and hoses. If you are compelled to take a "Lie Detector" test as a pre-requisite for employment, or in the course of a police interrogation or a court trial, there are some things that you simply MUST know in order to protect yourself from this type of techno-quackery. You need to go to www.polygraph.com and learn how these machines "work", and what they can and cannot "detect".

This book is about *becoming* a "lie detector" – a *human* lie detector. We will set forth here some 60+ rules and axioms[3] in order to clarify the following techniques. The methodology presented here has been tested by the author, and found to be effective in a vast majority of various circumstances. When you finish reading this book, it will be difficult if not impossible for anyone to lie to you and get away with it for very long. Part of being a good investigator is being able to tell when someone is lying to you. The completion of competency in that regard is to have the ability to prove it. In short, that is the goal of this little book: to develop and fine tune those abilities in the reader; to make of him or her, not only a good detec*tor* but a detec*tive* that is ultimately able to get to the truth of a matter. The development of those abilities, I have found, do not depend so much on formal "detective training",[4] as it does on the way that one thinks about what is said to him when he/she makes inquiries into the facts of a particular matter.

Human thought processes are dependent upon concepts, which in turn are comprised of the various definitions and paradigms[5] that one acquires by the experiences of life. One will rarely have a set of codified[6] definitions upon which to base his reasoning, and therefore the efforts expended to get at the truth of a matter are often quite futile, or at least,

---

[2] Polygraph Machine – an electronic graphing recorder that measures heart rate, respiration, and skin conductivity. Commonly called a "Lie Detector", the machine cannot detect lies, or verify truth. Polygraph operators are all charlatans, and there is no "science" at all to this quack technology.

[3] Axiom - a law that is on the level of a physical science.

[4] *i.e.*: a formal school or a course that one could take.

[5] Paradigm - pre-conceived notion / way of thinking.

[6] Codified - exactly defined in writing, systematic; completely documented.

frustrating. Logical reasoning cannot coexist with emotion; the two are mutually exclusive; "emotion" being defined as an "unthinking reaction" as opposed to a logical response. We will cover this as well.

The object here is to develop a healthy skepticism without crossing the line into paranoia; it is a fine line, indeed. Since the abilities we seek to develop are in reality inter-dependent, the concepts and methods are not presented in any particular order. The axioms are a foundation that we will build upon in the opening chapters; the application of the rest of what is presented will depend upon the various situations to which it is applied.

Each of the elements or axioms is to some extent, dependent upon the others, and so all of them should be considered in order to get the full impact of what is presented. Examples are given in a few cases, but you will no doubt, find many more of your own that you can more easily relate to. You are encouraged to take notes, and develop some of your own "rules" as you read here. In the end, the desired result will be an enhanced ability to discern fact from fiction, and the inability to be fooled (for long) will develop.

While it is true that none of us tell the truth 100% of the time, a majority of the everyday untruth does not involve the avoidance or deception surrounding intentional, harmful, or what we will call "oppressive acts", or "Overts".[7] We will define "a lie" completely, so that the concept is developed fully, primarily in order that we aren't carried away in unfounded witch-hunts; such is the province of the courts and the media, along with aspiring politicians with a sensationalist agenda. Once you get past the chapter on cognitive dissonance,[8] you'll be able to spot them immediately. To begin with, I will list my "collection" of axioms, in no special order, except those that I feel presented first, will aid in the understanding of those that follow. Some of them have been "borrowed" from Scientology[9] as indicated. They are numbered for later reference in the following chapters.

---

[7] Overt – Dianetics / Scientology term used throughout as a pronoun – a transgression, offense, or sinful act or act of omission.

[8] Dissonance - see the chapter on Cognitive Dissonance for a complete definition.

[9] Scientology - an applied religious philosophy based on Dianetics. See: www.scientology.org

FOREWORD

By: David Todeschini

This work was spawned in the cauldron; in the Devil's workshop of the New York State prison system, where one could observe an interminable litany of liars at their perfected art every day; a place where lies are a codified science. The ironic truth is that *I'm **not** talking about the prisoners.* One must be careful with this technology. It will change how you think about what people say to you. It will open your eyes and help you detect the "smoke" before it obscures the truth forever. Once you read this book, you will look at the NEWS, political speeches, reasons for going to war and media reports of "crime out-of-control" in an entirely new light. One has to wonder, for example, whether the incidence of crime in our schools was preceded by the introduction of psychologists and social workers, or whether it is the other way around. The following quote might be of interest in the clarification of this issue:

"Schools will become clinics whose purpose is to provide individualized psycho-social treatment for the student, and teachers must become psycho-social therapists. This will include bio-chemical and psychological mediation of learning, as drugs are introduced experimentally to improve in the learner such qualities as personality, concentration, and memory. Children are to become the objects of experimentation". [10]
                                          - NEA report on "Education in the '70s"

Invariably, ethics, morality, conscience, and man's nature turn up in the discussion. I do not apologize for mentioning God or quoting a few scriptures. I'm sorry if that offends you secular humanists,[11] Darwinists,[12] and Evolutionists.[13] <u>God</u> created <u>me</u>! If you believe that you come from a monkey "down the tree" somewhere, speak for yourself. I pity you. Man did not "evolve", and the Earth is certainly <u>NOT</u> billions of years old. The Colorado River did <u>NOT</u> form Grand Canyon; it was cut out of soft mud by Noah's flood about 4,300 years ago. If you can prove "evolution", a small fortune awaits you.[14]

---

[10] Source: *"The Unseen Hand"* - Ralph Epperson ISBN # 0-9614135-06 - *Id* at 383.
[11] Secular humanists - those who believe that "man is god".
[12] Darwinists - those who believe that life "evolved" from lower life-forms.
[13] Evolutionists - Darwinists who believe that life "evolved" from non-life (ultimately from a rock).
[14] Kent Hovind, a Creation Science Evangelist offers a $250,000 reward for empirical proof of Darwinian-style "evolution". See: his web site at: http://www.drdino.com

In this book, I pull no punches. I make no attempt at *political correctness*. I do not have the reputation of being a diplomat. The truth hurts, but it will also set you free. Efficable technology is proven in the field. "Technology" that fails miserably is also so proven; it is then called "quackery" and eventually abandoned. If it is not abandoned, then it will cause no end to grief to those who are "willingly ignorant",[15] and refuse to change their views.

The reader can tell from reading this tome, and from examining other titles that I have authored,[16] that I am no great fan of the psychiatry profession. I have posted many scathing articles about this nefarious profession on my web site.[17] What is contained within this book is by no means, "psychiatry". Most psychiatrists couldn't find their ass with both hands, but they find numerous ways to swindle the taxpayers out of their hard-earned money.[18] Rather, what is contained within these pages arose mostly from dealing with people who boasted of credentials in this profession, but could never produce any tangible, meaningful, positive results by the application of their *"Ologia"*.[19]

But I digress....

No apologies. No Freudian psychobabble.[20] No "science" falsely so called.[21] just the truth.

DISCLAIMER: The author has studied Dianetics and Scientology extensively, but is NOT an active member of the Church of Scientology. The opinions, views, and methodologies presented herein, do not necessarily represent Dianetics, or The Church of Scientology; they are the author's views, which of course, must draw upon all of the author's knowledge and experience.

---

[15] "Willingly ignorant" - aka: "stupid on purpose" – see: 2 Peter 3:1-6 *KJV*

[16] Particularly *"A Synthesis of The Russian Brainwashing Manual on Psychopolitics"*, and *"Psychiatry, Mind Control, Genocide, and Infanticide"*. See my web site at: www.Net4TruthUSA.com or my bookstore at: www.LuLu.com/Net4TruthUSA.

[17] See the "Page 57" section – www.Net4TruthUSA.com/Page57.htm

[18] I have exposed several psychiatric swindles; one was a VA nurse pretending to be a psychiatrist who "treated" prisoners in an upstate NY prison (DVA IG case # 2001-HL-0066), and the others were real Ph. Ds who scammed the Medicare system (as a confidential informant for the NY Attorney General - Medicare Fraud Control Unit).

[19] Ologia – (Greek) "knowledge" or "knowledge of".

[20] Psychobabble - psychiatric jargon that doesn't make sense.

[21] See: 1 Timothy 6:20 KJV translation.

THE AXIOMS[22]

Possibly, the best way to present this subject is to list the axioms first. Although you might not understand all of them at the outset, I believe it would be advantageous to become a bit familiar with the concepts and the unique terminology. References are given for the reader to do some follow-up study. Several of the following statements are taken from Scientology texts and are noted in the margin by the symbol ✳, and footnoted where necessary.

✳   1.   *"A lie is a second postulate,[23] statement, or condition designed to mask a primary postulate which is permitted to remain".[24]*
- Scientology axiom # 36

A corollary:

✳   1c.   *"A lie is a second postulate designed to mask a primary postulate, statement, or condition which is permitted to remain".*

2.   A lie is told to conceal a harmful, suppressive[25] act, or to hide a painful or embarrassing truth.

3.   If a harmful or suppressive act is known to have been committed, then there will arise somewhere, the inevitable lie or second postulate or statement designed to conceal it.

✳   4.   *"In order for anything to persist, it must contain a lie* [or false data]*".[26]* - Scientology axiom # 38 - *Ibid.*

5.   A relevant truth or fact withheld or concealed is a lie or second postulate of omission.

---

[22] Axiom - a law that is on the level of a physical science.
[23] Postulate - a conclusion, decision, or resolution; thinkingness with intent to act.
[24] *"What Is Scientology"* – Id at 657- Bridge Publications – ISBN 1-57318-122-6 see: www.bridgepub.com
[25] Suppressive - an action that prevents another from acting / affecting.
[26] *"What Is Scientology"* - Id at 658 – Bridge Publications – ISBN 1-57318-122-6 see: www.bridgepub.com

6.   In order to believe a lie, one must first stop believing the truth; and once you stop believing the truth, it is then quite possible that you will believe anything.

7.   Faith is not so much a leap in the dark as it is resting in the sufficiency of the evidence.

8.   "The danger with the use of circumstantial evidence is that of logical gaps; subjective,[27] inferential[28] links of low probability, or insufficient degree".[29] - *People vs. Cleague 22 NY2d 363, 367, 292*

9.   A liar will tell you anything he thinks you are gullible, naïve, ignorant, or stupid enough to believe.

10.   He who lies first is usually believed instead of one who tells the truth second, or in response to (in defense of) the lie.

11.   When dealing with liars, one must realize that nothing at all may actually be, as it appears to be.

12.   The complexity of a lie or the number of second postulates is directly proportional to the severity of the offense that is concealed thereby.

13.   A person who will lie about a small thing will also lie about matters that are more important.

14.   If a lie is big enough and told boldly enough, people are likely to believe it without question. - Adolph Hitler (paraphrased)

15.   A thief is invariably a liar, because the fact that the theft occurred must be withheld; the commission of any harmful or suppressive act makes one a liar by omission or commission, because the Overt[30] must be concealed.

---

[27] Subjective - having to do only with theory or speculation.
[28] Inferential - an allegation of inference by leading the listener to draw conclusions from selected data presented to him/her.
[29] This is quoted from the legal case cited.
[30] Overt – Dianetics / Scientology term used throughout as a pronoun – a transgression, offense, or sinful act or omission.

16.   A lie told by the NEWS media becomes the Gospel truth.

17.   A half-truth is equal to a covert negative;[31] it is still a lie.

18.   Lies are more likely to be believed when the liar can evoke sympathy, empathy, pity, or compassion in the listener.[32]

19.   All politicians and elected officials, as well as lawyers, are pathological[33] liars.[34]

✳   20.   *There's always a hidden (undiscovered) third party that is telling lies and instigating[35] or creating enmity[36] that is the cause of every dispute.* (In Scientology, this is called "The Third-Party Law" – paraphrased).

21.   Lies breed tertiary[37] postulates when suspected or discovered.

22.   The collateral data that surrounds secondary or tertiary postulates becomes increasingly confusing and irrelevant.

23.   Man is prone to engage in witch-hunts.

✳   24.   *When people do not have all the facts of a matter, they will invent them. This is called "dub-in".[38]*

✳   25.   *"Anyone giving two contrary facts becomes a prime suspect for further investigation".[39]*

---

[31] Covert negative – a hidden negative or disparaging statement usu. implied and not articulated.

[32] This is why allegations of rape or child molestation (true or not) are impossible to defend against.

[33] Pathological liars - people who lie for the sake of lying; even when it would be better to tell the truth.

[34] As far as I can determine, there is no exception to this rule: ALL politicians & elected officials are LIARS.

[35] Instigating - to provoke a conflict between people.

[36] Enmity – To make enemies; to instigate feelings of ill will.

[37] Tertiary – third. Primary=1, secondary=2, tertiary=3, etc.

[38] "Dub-in" - a phenomenon wherein the mind "fills in" missing data in a memory in order to add context to an event. Aka: "false memory syndrome".

[39] *"What Is Scientology"* – Id at 681 - ISBN 1-57318-122-6 Bridge Publications www.bridgepub.com

26.   A string of inconsistencies is reliable *indicia*[40] that prior postulates or statements are lies; *i.e.:* the respondent to a series of questions is attempting to conceal a fact, or set of facts.

27.   Taking "The Fifth Amendment" is tacit[41] admission of guilt in a matter; the suspect is avoiding making second postulates or statements that when proven to be false, would impugn[42] his entire testimony. It is *prima facie*[43] *indicia* that the person being questioned most definitely has something to hide. Legally, invoking the 5th is NOT an admission of guilt, but the effect is nonetheless an admission of culpability in the eyes of a judge and jury.

28.   It is impossible for more than one person to keep lies consistent. A group of liars concealing the same Overt[44] will be inconsistent with the collateral facts that are common among them; the amount of inconsistency rises exponentially with each new member of a "liar's club".

29.   There's no such thing as an "impartial", or "unbiased" witness.

30.   People (especially children)[45] can be brainwashed.

31.   A libel or slander, which is believed without question, is the functional equivalent of an empirical[46] truth.

32.   The testimony of two witnesses who do not know each other and could not have conspired together, which reveals identical facts or similar situations must be considered factual. If more than three or four such witnesses arise, their combined testimony is irrefutable, even if the facts or events in question seem "fantastic". But then again it may be corroboration with intent to deceive if too many small details of their stories match perfectly – especially if they are articulated verbatim.

---

[40] Indicia – (Latin) indication.
[41] Tacit – understood without being spoken; implied.
[42] Impugn – to raise an objection concerning a thing's voracity.
[43] Prima facie – (Latin, legal term) "on its face".
[44] Overt – Dianetics / Scientology term used throughout as a pronoun – a transgression, offense, or sinful act or omission.
[45] Children normally cannot assert themselves over the insistence of a recognized authority figure.
[46] Empirical – derived from direct experience; testable; verifiable; surviving practical tests of verity.

33.   Truth is easy to remember – it will be consistent with the passage of time, although more detail will emerge in questioning or processing.[47] Lies are the polar opposite. Lies are hard to remember, and they will become more inconsistent as conflicting details emerge with further questioning.

34.   Two opposing facts or postulates cannot both be true. A direct contradiction of postulates causes a paradox;[48] in legal terms: antimony.[49] Logic dictates that one or both is false, or at the very least, not an exact consideration. This condition existing in the case that any significant statement supports a "fact" that is subsequently found to be a lie, is reliable *indicia* of the probable presence of layers of second postulates.

35.   Anyone found to be fabricating lies; second or tertiary postulates, or aiding and abetting same, must be considered as a suspect in the commission of the harmful or suppressive act being concealed, or at least by tacit consent as being party to it (and culpable for it).

36.   A question, the answer to which if truthful, should be innocuous or harmless to the person being questioned if he is innocent. When the question is avoided or answered with a lie, the answer is a postulate or statement that is other than the primary postulate, statement, or condition which is *"the exact consideration"* or truth of the matter. The reason for the avoidance of the question, or the lie in response to it, once discovered, brings one a step closer to the empirical truth.

37.   An investigator who does not question the verity[50] or voracity[51] of a statement or response to a question is unwittingly leading a witness to make second or tertiary postulates that if believed, will contaminate a case with false data, causing the case to persist.

38. A lie or second postulate, which mitigates[52] the cognitive dissonance of the listener, will be instantly believed.

---

[47] The "processing" referred to here is Dianetics auditing, not psychoanalysis (which is worse than useless).
[48] Paradox – reasoning that offends against logic.
[49] Antimony - (legal term) a paradox caused by a contradiction.
[50] Verity – a piece of true information.
[51] Voracity – a desire to excess – common usage denotes insistence; strength of a statement.
[52] Mitigate – to lessen the severity of the impact of a matter; to make less severe.

A corollary:

38c.   Truth being spoken imparts relevance to the available facts of the case, and will also mitigate cognitive dissonance by causing the case to *unmock*,[53] or not persist.

※   39.   *Data or the facts of a case are only as valuable as they are evaluated, and are only as important as it serves to clarify other data, or impart relevance or importance to other facts.*[54]
- Scientology Logics #9 and #10 combined, paraphrased

40.   The opposite of a lie is an *exact consideration* or series of such considerations, which seeks to impart relevance to all the applicable collateral data and facts of the case.

41.   Unevaluated or improperly evaluated data or facts, whose proper relationship to known, true data, physical evidence (solid matter) or objective direct observation that has not been established, is functionally and for all practical purposes, equivalent to an undiscovered lie, a withheld statement, truth, or fact.

42.   A lie told by a credible witness is by definition, "*believable*"; it is nonetheless a lie.

43.   It is easier for a credible witness to lie and be believed, than it is for the average man to similarly deceive.

44.   A credible witness who lies, and is never caught lying, increases his credibility by the very lie he/she tells, when they are not exposed as lies.

45.   A credible witness who lies and is believed, is the functional equivalent of a pathological liar.

46.   Lies or false statements, libel, or slander which has absolutely no basis or foundation in fact, quickly escalates to the level limited only by the imagination and the surrounding circumstances.

---

[53] *Unmock* - a Scientology term - meaning to "fall apart" or "un-ravel".
[54] *"What Is Scientology"* – *Id* at 635 - Bridge Publications – ISBN 1-57318-122-6 see: www.bridgepub.com

47.   Out of the mouths of babes or imbeciles, filtered through the thinkingness[55] and embellishment of a psychiatrist, psychologist, therapist, social worker, or other various and sundry *Hick-Farmer Sigmund Freud Wannabes,*[56] come the most incredible and fantastic bullshit stories ever to be conceived in the mind of man.[57]

48.   A "psychological profile" is the chief method by which innocent people can be blamed for and found guilty of a crime or harmful or suppressive acts they did not commit; all are second postulates and theories that have nothing to do with facts, but are believed to be true.

49.   A liar will not lie unless he thinks he will be believed, while a pathological liar will not consider the likelihood of being **dis**believed, because he believes the lie himself. The pathological liar is "cool", because he reasons that he can always make tertiary postulates or statements to explain why the second postulate or statement should be believed, if he should be exposed.

50.   A pathological liar will convey an untruth as a matter of habit if the verity of the matter in question is not self-evident to the questioner – or – if the liar knows that the investigator already knows the truth.

51.   Even a "good" pathological liar is rarely consistent over time about his "facts". Given enough liberty to do so, he will attempt to gain credibility with layers of second postulates that will inevitably contradict each other, or form a chain of *non-sequiturs*[58] that are readily discernible as lies.

---

[55] Thinkingness - the state of one's reasoning processes; the "state of cognition".

[56] Hick-Farmer Sigmund Freud Wannabes – (coined phrase by the author) refers to social workers and Department of Social
      Services (DSS) employees, and "therapists" in general who are not Scientologists.
      See research papers on http://home.earthlink.net/~rkmck/vault/reprints/bruceci95ab.html and reports on false allegations of "Ritual Abuse" on http://www.religioustolerance.org/child3.htm
      Quoting the latter research: *"This study is believed to be the first one of its type involving many dozens of children who were interviewed over long periods of time. It shows the dangers of repeated and suggestive questioning of children. It demonstrates how easy it is to obtain disclosures from children of sexual abuse events that never happened. It sheds doubt on the use of body diagrams and anatomically correct dolls. It seems to indicate the extreme unreliability of suggestive, closed, and persistent questioning".*

[58] *Non-sequituer* - (Latin, legal term) - "it does not follow".

14

52.   What is commonly called "denial" is not a lie *per se '*; it is in fact, the inability[59] to confront a painful or embarrassing truth.

53.   A person upon being confronted with false data that cannot be disproven suffers dissonance. He will employ Asserted Rightness[60] in order to be right, and the case will persist.

54.   "Denial" becomes a lie (or a "Withhold"[61]) when it seeks to conceal a crime (or Overt[62]) that is ongoing, and/or for which one could be punished, penalized, or prosecuted.

55.   If you keep asking a question long enough, inevitably you will be told exactly what you want to hear.[63] Unfortunately, you will have imposed your own conclusions or "hypothesized cues" over the evidence and facts, and the case will persist (not resolve) as a result.

✳   56.   *"That which you validate will come true".*[64]

A corollary:

56c.   That which you validate will become a self-fulfilling prophesy.

57.   Truth can be anything you want it to be.[65] Imposing your conclusions by force or coercion upon another person evokes a conflict of Asserted Rightness.[66] The case will persist (not be solved).

---

[59] This "inability" is beyond the person's volitional control, and is, in fact, a natural and mentally healthy response, attempting to "distance himself" from the commission of crime or offensive act which caused harm or trauma. Psychiatry and Psychology insist that the opposite is true, and attempt to hold their patients in the "valence" of the personality, which committed the Overt. The person then has the cognition that in order to be right, he has to assert his "rightness"; i.e.: that the offense was innocuous. He asserts his "rightness" (justification) by repeating the behavior.

[60] Asserted Rightness - a condition where the ASSERTION of "being right" takes precedence over the truth.

[61] Withhold - used here as a pronoun - a fact or a bit of knowledge intentionally withheld or concealed; a lie of omission.

[62] Overt – Dianetics / Scientology term used throughout as a pronoun – a transgression, offense, or sinful act or omission.

[63] See the chapter on "Ally Computation" for an explanation of this phenomenon.

[64] Dianetics - Research & Discovery series (Oct 1951) vol. 9, - *Id* at 22 ¶6 - ISBN 0-88404-183-2

[65] In reality, "truth" is a statement that comports to reality, but "truth" - especially in court, is often, tragically, a matter of consensus of opinion.

[66] Asserted Rightness - a condition where the ASSERTION of "being right" takes precedence over the truth.

58. "Once one accepts a logical contradiction, one can prove anything one likes – it is the end of rational thought". [67]

59 "When you change the way you look at things, the things you are looking at, change".[68]

60. "Once you've learned to lie to yourself, lying to others becomes the natural thing to do". – Honor Bound Magazine,[69] Winter 2003

61. An investigator cannot argue with his or her own conclusions. If an investigator (or a person asking questions) can be manipulated into coming to the wrong conclusion by a skillful liar (or propaganda team), the lies that the respondent to questioning tells will be believed. This technique works because it extinguishes the dissonance in the investigator's mind. The longer the deception is believed, the less likely it is that the truth will ever be discovered.

62. People who cannot or will not "connect the dots" when they clearly are astute and intelligent enough to do so, usually fail to "connect the dots" because they **ARE** the "dots".

※ 63. *"The workability of a postulate is established by the degree to which it explains existing phenomena [which is] already known; by the degree that it predicts new phenomena which when looked for, will be found to exist, and by the degree that it does not require that phenomena which do not exist in fact, be called into existence for its explanation."* [70] - Scientology Logic #19

This is possibly the most useful and profound of all the axioms here.

64. The inability of a defendant to prove a negative, or to overcome the bias, prejudice, and / or corruption of a judge and jury, does not validate the charges against him as being true.

65. The persistent paucity of a statement or narrative is an **Orange Alert** that a lie is being told.

---

[67] The Cosmic Code - *Id* at 158, ¶1 - Simon & Schuster – ISBN 0671-24802-2

[68] Wayne Dyer *"The Power of Intention"* on WLIW-TV 9-12-04 (800) 767-2121

[69] Honor Bound Magazine – see: www.honorbound.com

[70] *"What Is Scientology?"* - *Id* at 636 - L. Ron Hubbard ISBN# 1-57318-122-6

66. Truth is a statement that comports to reality.

※   67. *"Stupidity is the unknowingness of consideration"*.

A corollary:

67c. Stupidity is the pursuit of ignorance.[71]

68.   "Even a liar tells a hundred truths to one lie; he has to, to make the lie good for anything".
> –   Henry Ward Beecher, American Clergyman (1813-1887)

69.   Do not substitute ANGER for EVIDENCE or confuse a VENDETTA for ENTHUSIASM.

There are probably many more axioms that can be added to the list; however, these will cover the vast majority of situations that you will encounter. Before you read any further, you should take the time to re-read this chapter, and try to relate each axiom to situations in your past experience, and make notes on your thoughts.

Also, before you proceed any further in the text that follows, it would be a good exercise to go through each of the preceding statements and make notes on how you would apply each of them to situations in people you encounter on a daily basis. When you have finished reading this book, go through your notes, and see how your approach to these things is changed.

Next, we will discuss lie detector machines, and then explore the concept of cognitive dissonance, and see how it relates to the investigation process.

---

[71] The Bible in 2 Peter Chapter 3, states that some people "willingly are ignorant". (Use KJV translation).

Lie Detectors - Polygraphs

To open this informative little essay, I will make an unequivocal[72] statement:

THERE IS NO SUCH THING AS A LIE DETECTOR.[73]

Such a machine does not exist in reality, and the more technically astute you are, the more you will realize that my statement above is an objective fact. A lengthy treatise on this topic here, is prohibitive, but I will touch on it briefly since the reader may encounter "lie detectors" at some point in his dealings with a corrupt government or an unscrupulous attorney. I will refer you instead, to reliable sources which qualify my claims here - experts in the field who will qualify what I tell you here as absolute fact.

"Lie Detectors" are really Polygraph machines. The word Polygraph comes from "poly" (many) and "graph" (drawing or chart). They measure heart rate (cardio), breathing (respiration), and skin resistance (sweating; galvanic). The machines themselves LOOK impressive, like a heart monitor or EKG[74] machine, but they are really "smoke and mirrors". The operator hides behind the apparency of technology when he asks you a set of questions that you will get to see in advance, and perhaps even propose yourself. The operator then "interprets" the charts, but in reality, the charts have little to do with anything. Whether you're lying or telling the truth, or whether you're nervous or afraid, apprehensive, or just embarrassed, the machine has no way of telling. The operator is the one who makes the ultimate decision.

Most States do not permit "Lie Detector Tests" as evidence in criminal cases. If you are technically knowledgeable, and you read the materials referenced (below), you will be able to "fool" any lie detector test, or so confound the results that the test will have to be called "inconclusive". Before you are hooked up to the machine, you will be given a brochure to read, which is written by the Polygrapher's Association of America or some-such impressive-sounding organization.

---

[72] Unequivocal – having a single, plain meaning.
[73] There is no such thing as a machine that can "detect" lies.
[74] EKG - Electrocardiogram – a trace recording of heart rhythms.

The literature will expound upon how "accurate" the machines are, and that at least, is a half-truth. The machines ARE accurate, precision instruments, which ACCURATELY record heart rate, respiration, and skin Galvanics,[75] but the accuracy of what the OBJECT of the measurements is supposed to indicate is in question. The brochure skillfully and covertly implies that the device is an accurate LIE DETECTOR, when the truth is; the machine is merely an accurate recorder of VITAL SIGNS.

A $4,000 polygraph machine had BEST be accurate in recording your heartbeat, respiration, and skin resistance - but accurate as those measurements may be, it has NOTHING to do with indicating whether you're lying or telling the truth (You could be nervous about failing the test, and if you <u>are</u>, you <u>will</u>).

Among the techniques that can be used to totally foil a "lie detector" test is taking a few tranquilizers an hour before. This will flatten your emotional response (flat affect), or by simply keeping your cool, since in most cases, you will know what the operator will ask you in advance. Of course, if you are a pathological liar (like most politicians), you will pass with flying colors, since pathological liars believe their own lies, and don't know they're lying. If you believe a lie, to YOU it's the truth! You won't get nervous, your heart won't "skip a beat", and you'll have the classic "poker face"; a "snow-job" so convincing, that the REAL "lie detector" - the polygraph operator, won't be able to tell that you're the biggest fibber since Fibber McGee.[76]

Another technique that reportedly works is verbalizing the lie, and answering with the truth in your head. For example, the polygraph operator asks "Did you murder *Joe Scarface Goomba*?" and you say "No" with your lips, but admit the crime saying "Yes, I did" to yourself in your head. Still another technique that has proven to work is "thought switching", where you imagine a different question than the question that is being asked, and you verbalize a TRUTHFUL answer to the imagined question.

---

[75] Galvanics – a measure of the skin's electrical conductivity – i.e.: how easily the skin passes electrical currents. Conductivity is the opposite of resistance (to current flow).
[76] Or Bill Clinton – (George Bush makes Clinton's lies seem like child's play; Clinton pales in comparison).

More advanced techniques involve biasing the "control baseline" - the measurements taken to a set of "control" questions that are asked prior to the pertinent questions, in order for the operator to "calibrate" the machine. Basically, you can manipulate the calibration of the polygraph by such things as wiggling your toes, tightening your sphincter muscles, in combination with certain mental imagery, and then telling the truth even if it incriminates you (it will be "interpreted" as a lie, or vice-versa). With the baseline calibration biased, the machine will indicate no abnormal reaction when you get nervous and lie, and you will pass the test.

Of course, if you are convinced (as well as you will be by reading the referenced materials), there will be no reason to be nervous, since you'll know that **THERE IS NO SUCH THING AS A LIE DETECTOR MACHINE.**

Of course, there is a bit more to these techniques than I can describe here, and they require a bit of practice. I will refer you to the referenced materials[77] to learn more. This book will teach you how <u>YOU</u> can become a "lie detector"… without investing $3,000 to $4,500 in a "polygraph" machine. If you care to donate or tithe[78] the money you'll save… well, you know where to send it.

Jefferson's (early) Polygraph machine (anybody need a mouse trap?)

---

[77] *"Introduction to Psychology"* - Dennis Coon - page 303-305 - ISBN # 0-8299-0134-5 West Publishing Co.
    Also see: www.polygraph.com - This web site is run by an ex-CIA agent with over 30 years of experience as a Polygrapher. If you will be taking a "lie detector" test anytime soon, you MUST visit his web site and obtain his book on how to fool the "lie detector".

[78] Tithe – a ten percent share of one's gross earnings, usually donated to a church or synagogue.

Sticks and Stones

A little girl once wrote on the blackboard:

"Sticks and stones may break my bones,
But words can break my heart."

The profound truth[79] is often forthcoming "out of the mouths of babes",[80] and whoever it was that wrote those words, sure put the second premise of that old saying into the light of day; she exposed the fallacy of ages, that words... *"Mere words cannot hurt us"*. This bit of wisdom ought to be rendered in neon lights and proclaimed on the electronic marquees in Times Square.

How many times in our lives have all of us hurt someone - cut them to the quick[81] with a cross word, started a rumor, or told a lie; and how easily do these things become embellished in the re-telling, until it gets completely out of context, out of proportion, and out of control!

Once told, it seems that lies take on a life of their own, but the lies are not easy to maintain for very long. It often takes more energy to maintain a falsehood than to tell the truth to begin with, and be done with it. The converse is true for the listener; it is easier to believe a lie and be done with it, than it is to seek after the truth and labor over uncovering it.

It is a natural fact, that human beings in general, do not like to work - mentally or physically - and that fact gives rise to the propensity to accept lies as truth, especially from those in position of authority. The government in general, and particularly the government and the media, since through our tax dollars and buying of sponsor's products, we pay them to discern "the truth" for us. It never crosses our minds that people who are assumed to be credible by the positions they have attained may in fact, be pathological liars,[82] or have agendas that are not consistent with the general welfare.

---

[79] And the most fantastic fantasies and outright lies.
[80] Psalms 8:2; Matthew 11:25; Luke 10:21
[81] Quick (Archaic) – muscle or sinew tissue.
[82] A pathological liar often believes his own lies to be true.

The Bible tells us: *"A false witness shall not be unpunished, and he that speaketh lies shall not escape."* - Proverbs 19:9

"Their throat is as an open sepulcher;[83] with their tongues they have used deceit; the poison of asps[84] is under their lips." - Romans 3:13

My Military Intelligence training taught me that although we could not prove a lie or a falsehood directly, we could discern the truth by examining the verity[85] of collateral[86] facts. In other words: *"I can't tell if you're lying, but I can tell whether you're lying when you say that you're telling me the truth."* The technique that is routinely used by interrogators who are vigilant and motivated to uncover the truth is to ask a question to which they already have the answer. If the subject lies about the collateral issues, then he is also, most certainly lying about the facts, or the veracity of his testimony is questionable.

If you've never studied Shakespeare, or seen the play *"Othello"*, then you've missed a truly classic example of how even an obvious lie, rendered with cunning and malice aforethought, can be seeded into the mind of someone (Othello) who is just a bit insecure in his marriage. This lie causes him such agony and jealousy that he ends up suffocating his lovely wife (Desdemona), who was, in truth, innocent of the allegations of infidelity and faithfully devoted to him.

When you stop and think, many of the fantastic bullshit stories we've been told by our government and the media over the years, all come unraveled once you pull on the metaphorical "loose thread". For example, the "lone gunman" conclusion of the Warren Commission report on the JFK assassination falls apart on several out-points.[87] Bullets do not stop in mid-air, and a man's head moves <u>forward</u> when the bullet strikes from the rear, not backwards. On that alone, anyone who has studied physics in high school would discount the "magic bullet" theory as total nonsense. My book *"Land of Childhood's Fears"* covers the JFK assassination and the Vietnam War from an entirely new perspective.

---

[83] Sepulcher - A tomb or grave.

[84] Asp – a poisonous snake.

[85] Verity – Truth.

[86] Facts that surround an issue or event.

[87] Out-point - a term in Scientology to designate a piece of data which is not consistent with the established empirical facts.

UFO's are another story entirely; the Air Force's "Project Blue Book" is another rambling pile of psycho-babble-bullshit that fails to explain the government's obvious fuss and secrecy over the crash of an expendable "weather balloon" in the New Mexico desert (balloons don't normally "crash"; they develop leaks and slowly come back down). It failed to explain the thousands of photos and videotapes taken of these things for over 60 years. Yes, some are hoaxes, which leaves us with the conclusion that most of them are **NOT** hoaxes.

The numerous cases of mysterious deaths of over 100 people who came forward with information about the JFK assassination, and over 70 people who had close ties to President Clinton; Vincent Foster in particular, do not make forensic sense to a person who is astute enough to cull the facts from the fiction. The law has a set of doctrines or axioms upon which the theory of jurisprudence[88] in the US is based. One such axiom is in the Latin: *"Falsus in uno, falsus in omnibus"* - False in one, false in all - and it goes back to the test of collateral facts. The *"uno"*, or "one" of the axiom, should ideally be a significant fact of the case, such as the known behavior of a bullet in flight, and what would inevitably happen to that bullet after it had crashed through a man's skull.

Certainly, there is NO WAY that it (the "magic" bullet) could be found in pristine condition. Moreover, how convenient that the most infamous murder weapon in modern history escaped the police chain of custody, and the defendant was murdered before he could have a chance to raise a defense. Once that false significant *"uno"* is found, if the rest of the case is built upon the *"uno"* being true, and the *"uno"* is NOT true, then the entire stack of lies falls apart.

The "energy" required to keep a lie going is enormous, and the effort to dig the truth out of a mountain of lies is exponentially greater. This is precisely why the American people have all but given up demanding the truth... too much energy has to be expended, the expending of energy is work, and time spent working takes away from the time spent in more enjoyable, albeit useless pursuits.[89]

---

[88] Jurisprudence - the code of laws.
[89] Useless persuits such as spectator sports in this country, and indeed the world as a whole, have become a multi billion dollar industry. Spectator sports are the true "opiate of the masses".

It is easy to see why this situation has become what it is today. When a question is asked, we either get a song and a tap-dance, or we get some more sugarcoated bullshit to cover up the previous lie. No matter what, the lies must be preserved at all costs, and the second or tertiary postulates are an insult to our intelligence.

The case of Agent Orange is a prime example. The US has used this stuff and knowingly made our own troops deathly sick as far back as the Korean War. Eventually, though, the truth emerges. It is surprising that nothing is ever done to bring the liars to justice. The American people leave these people in office, apparently content to have their legs peed on, and be told, "It's raining".[90] It is obviously easier to believe a lie than to labor over truth, and we will cover precisely WHY shortly. Collectively, the American people have elected to take the path of least resistance by not calling the liars to task, even when the truth is glaringly obvious, because the lies are glaringly obvious to anyone but an idiot.

Lies, no matter what, should not be tolerated, and in my book on Vietnam,[91] I document just some of the effects of the government's lies upon the American people, and on the brave young men and women who had served honorably in an unpopular war; the "ten thousand day war" of Vietnam. There is nothing that can be done about Vietnam now; it is *"water under the bridge"*, but through my book, I hope to educate America, so that the protracted agony of the only war America ever lost, does not get a repeat performance in the Middle East. It is a pity that Shakespearian literature is too often taken as "entertainment", and hardly ever taken to heart for its moral lessons. It is also a shame that the only nation on the planet that has ever proclaimed its unity "Under God", now disavows any knowledge of His actions or His words... some deny that God even exists, and prefer to believe the outright lunacy of *"Big Bangs"*, Vacuum Genesis, and Darwinian evolution. My God, man! - We've gone insane!

Read on and learn how to extract yourself from the national insanity, by knowing when you're being taken for a sucker.

---

[90] See *"Don't Pee On My Leg And Tell Me It's Raining"* - by Judge Judy Shiendlin - ISBN# 0-06-092794-1
[91] *"Land of Childhood' Fears - Faith, Friendship, and The Vietnam War"* – See: www.Net4TruthUSA.com

COGNITIVE DISSONANCE FACTOR

I may seem to have bombarded the reader with a host of axioms and definitions (over 68 thus far, not counting the corollaries) but please bear with me; the following will tie most of the axioms together with "common threads".

Cognitive dissonance theory is perhaps one concept in the study of psychology that has any validity to it. However, because pursuit of the line of reasoning that dissonance theory leads to, takes us into the realm of man's spirituality (something that psychology tries to deny), cognitive dissonance theory is largely abandoned in the field of psychology today:

"Cognitive dissonance is a motivational or negative drive state [of mind] *which is aroused when a person simultaneously holds two cognitions[92] that are inconsistent with each other... is an uncomfortable state of arousal or tension which individuals are motivated to reduce... produced... by inconsistency between an individual's behavior and self-concept".[93]*   (Brackets mine)

Related to this, is the dissonance that drives a person to ask questions. A question arises when a person's "cognitions" are at odds with each other. When the question is answered to the investigator's satisfaction (accepted as true), the dissonance no longer exists, and there's no need to ask any more questions; the situation is resolved in the mind of the questioner.

From this, our axiom #38 and #38c arose. How dissonance plays a role in the investigation process is very important to understand; it marks the difference between an investigator who gets to the truth of a matter by the application of knowledge and skill, and a mere "Gumshoe" [94] who may only discover the half of it by physically and mentally exhausting himself with a blind persistence. This point is so important, that it merits its own chapter, and an example of it that follows:

---

[92] Cognition – the activity of the mind; thoughts, conclusions, etc.
[93] See: *"Trauma Victim"* - Lee Hyer, *et.al.* - *Id* at 685, 686 - ISBN 1-55959-047-5 (out-of-print).
[94] Gumshoe - archaic slang for "detective" or "investigator".

November 22, 1963 – Dallas, Texas – John Fitzgerald Kennedy, one of the nation's best-loved presidents is assassinated in broad daylight as his motorcade rolls through a crowd of thousands of spectators. Immediately following the NEWS broadcasts America and the world are in a state of shock and disbelief. The reality of the situation made itself felt, and the public, quite understandably, wanted the shooter or shooters caught and executed. Forty years later, we know little more of what transpired that day than we did then; we know that the CIA actually had JFK killed, and set up Lee Harvey Oswald as the "Fall Guy".[95] However, let's look back at the events of that day and the days following, and evaluate the public's reaction.

It would probably be safe to say that the dissonance of the public was aroused, in that the "drive" to find the killer (or to know he / they had been caught) had to be satisfied. When Oswald was arrested *that very same day*, and said to be "a suspect", the entire world would have lynched him on the spot, without a shred of tangible evidence to tie him to the crime. Following Oswald's arrest, which was probably part of the assassination plan, in retrospect we have possibly the fastest criminal investigation in US history. The subsequent bullshit story with the pristine bullet[96] found on a gurney in the hospital, and that the rifling marks matched the Manlikker-Carcano[97] rifle (allegedly) registered to Oswald, was never proven in court. In fact, the Warren Commission came up with their own second and tertiary postulates; the public, eager to have resolution of the matter, believed it. It is tragic, but in light of much new evidence that has since come to light, a majority of the public *still* believe that Oswald was the "*lone gunman*", because it is easier to cling to that belief, than to revive that state of dissonance and "not know" once again. This brings us to the realization that:

#57 - "Truth can be anything you want it to be", and
#23 - "Man is prone to engage in witch-hunts".

---

[95] See: my books: *"Land of Childhood's Fears"* and *"Vet's Rap Sessions"* on www.Net4TruthUSA.com and also: "First-Hand Knowledge"- by Robert Morgan.

[96] Pristine bullet – looks as if it never hit anything solid, or was fired into a bale of cotton. Bullets that are fired – even through soft flesh, are always damaged in the impact. The bullet found on the gurney in Parkland Hospital was planted, or the story was a deception.

Manlikker Carcano – a cheap Italian-made bolt-action rifle that could NOT be capable of the accuracy required for the shots alleged to have been fired in such rapid sequence. For a digital simulation of the JFK assassination. See: www.JFKReloaded.com

The fact that the assassination was planned by the CIA – and because the public was led to believe that Oswald was the "lone gunman", proves that:

#30 - "People... can be brainwashed".

Lee Harvey Oswald was convicted in the public's mind because of the "profiling" done by the police and the FBI.

#48 - "a "psychological profile" is the method by which innocent people can be blamed and found guilty of a crime... they did not commit..."

Therefore, we see that at least in the JFK case, that presumption of innocence and all the tenets of Constitutional and civil liberties that we hold dear, were effectively made moot. The due process of law[98] was simply done away with by Jack Ruby, who shot Oswald on live TV, "In front of God and everybody",[99] in the basement of the Dallas police station. In retrospect, the lies were incredible, and still, we have not seen the autopsy photos that would show that the direction from which the (magic) bullet(s)[100] came, was from the front. Axioms #34 and #36 apply. The lesson to be learned here, is that the JFK assassination investigation ended where it did, not so much because of corruption or incompetence, but because the public found it easier to trust their government's credibility (see axioms #42 to #45) than to allow facts (physical evidence) into the equation. Most people are ignorant of the science of ballistics,[101] and had the public been shown what typically happens to a lead bullet after you shoot it into a human being,[102] there would not have been all of the tertiary postulates that followed. A good tool to learn more about how the public was lied to is to play a digital simulation of the JFK assassination available on the web site: www.JFKReloaded.com.

---

[98] Due process of law is "guaranteed" by the 14th Amendment of the US Constitution.

[99] *"In front of God and everybody"* – meaning that the person does (did) not care who observed the act.

[100] The bullet was called "magic" because it sustained no damage, and (according to the Warren Commission) defied the laws of physics and ballistics.

[101] Ballistics - the science of studying the behavior of projectiles.

[102] A bullet shot into a human body, flattens and mushrooms, and no longer resembles "a bullet" to the untrained eye.

As an investigator after empirical[103] truth, you cannot accept a bit of theory that does not make sense of all the relevant facts – and physical evidence cannot be ignored. All of that was done in the JFK investigation, and the ensuing Warren Commission hearings. Competent investigators cannot afford to coddle their cognitive dissonance with bogus "facts" or assumptions that are not supported by some sort of physical evidence. The "facts" must pass all the tests. "Professional" liars such as politicians and intelligence agents are very skilled at determining what will resolve dissonance in an inquisitor's mind, and arranging it so that the investigator "retrieves" the information via "his own efforts", and then arrives at conclusions that are entirely rational. (An investigator is unlikely to argue with his or her own conclusions – see Axiom # 61).

Skilled Psy-Ops[104] operatives are adept at creating "facts" and misinformation that cause the listener (in this case, the American Public) to come to wrong conclusions with the right data. Thinking that the conclusion is his (their) own, the objects of this technology never question the conclusion, because they believe the conclusion to be a product of their own thoughts.[105] This removes the liar from the loop, and focuses (diverts) the investigator's attention elsewhere.

Another technique used by scam artists, primarily, is to set up a situation so that an embezzlement scheme for example, can be made to look like a "bookkeeping error" instead of what it really is. If the scam gets discovered before the perpetrators can get their hands on the cash, the "mistake" can be corrected and at least nobody goes to jail.

It is far better to suffer an "ass-reaming" by the boss, than an extended trip to the Hoosegow.[106] It is by far, best that one "cop a plea" to being incompetent, than to deny culpability, and be accused of sedition and treason.[107]

---

[103] Empirical – derived from direct experience; testable; verifiable; surviving practical tests of verity.

[104] Psy-Ops – (military term) – Psychological Operations.

[105] I discussed this phenomenon on the July 2, 2004 Radio Liberty program titled "Operation Phoenix". You can download the entire 2 hour interview or listen to other programs by logging on to my web site at www.Net4TruthUSA.com

[106] Hoosegow - slang term for "lock-up" - jail or prison, gaol.

[107] This is what the FBI did when accused of complicity in the 9-11 attacks. This is a standard Military Intelligence tactic. See my book: *Land of Childhood's Fears* about the Vietnam war, available on the bookstore on the web site at: www.Net4TruthUSA.com or www.LuLu.com/Net4TruthUSA

Suspicion is a condition of cognitive dissonance between an event that happened: a crime, missing money, dead bodies, etc. and the causes (or suspects) which are unknown. Dissonance is the motivator that drives one to seek a solution by asking questions. In the common vernacular, dissonance is the technical nomenclature[108] for that "instinct" that tells you *"Something ain't Kosher, here"*. Once an acceptable solution is found, dissonance is relieved, and there is no longer any need to investigate.

None of this is meant to imply that one should be constantly suspicious: However, an investigator must be careful to properly weigh the impact of words on his actions. If solid evidence exists that a crime or Overt[109] has been committed, then there is a lie, Withhold,[110] or a hidden fact somewhere, which seeks to conceal it (see axiom #3, #25, #36 and #39). If you have a suspect, gather up all the irrefutable facts first, and then question him only on the *out-points*[111] you already know the answers to. Give him the opportunity to lie, or to tell the truth.

If the suspect lies on key points of the matter, do not react, and do not pursue the matter any further at this time. If he tells the truth, it does not necessarily absolve him, or take him off the list of suspects, but it is perhaps, *indicia* that your time and energy might be better spent elsewhere at the present time. Return to the questioning of the suspect only when you have other empirical facts about which to inquire.

You should also be aware that politicians routinely propose a "solution" to a problem that they know will never work, but which a majority of people out of ignorance or outright stupidity, will allow themselves to believe.[112] They do this in order to have some solution (instead of none). I could think of several examples, but the most ludicrous of them all has to be the proposal by a New York State Gubernatorial candidate a decade or so ago, for requiring ammunition manufacturers to put serial numbers on (individual) bullets.

---

108 Nomenclature - the name or identification given to something.
109 Overt – Dianetics / Scientology term used throughout as a pronoun – a transgression, offense, or sinful act or omission.
110 Withhold - used here as a pronoun - a fact or a bit of knowledge intentionally withheld or concealed; a lie of omission.
111 Out-Point – a bit of data or a fact which does not "jibe" with the proven forensics or facts of a case.
112 For this they willingly are IGNORANT... II Peter 3:5 *KJV*.

The Lie Detection Manual

Now while it is technically and *actually possible* to put serial numbers on individual bullets, one has to ask what criminal in his right mind would use (or buy) serial-numbered bullets[113] and shoot somebody? Not many, I'd venture to speculate. Well, to some people, this "ingenious" idea would, if implemented, solve the problem of gun-related crime. Needless to say, we have very good data on how many imbeciles we have in New York by the tally of votes this man received.

By the way, Blaming guns for Columbine,[114] is like blaming spoons for Rosie O'Donnell being fat.

Politicians are all pathological liars (axiom #19). No one with any ounce of sense at all could possibly spend more than a minute to think about why serial numbers on bullets wouldn't work or would work and not call the idea "absurd". Here is an educated man who put much thought into his proposal, not because he thought it would work to benefit his constituents, but because he was relying on the ignorance and stupidity of the public at large. He tried to convince enough people that his plan would work, in order to be elected. It didn't work. The man never became Governor, we don't have serial numbers on bullets, and the crime problem is worse than ever... but it is *not* worse for the lack of serial-numbered bullets.

Ignorance is excusable – it is impossible for a person, or the general public to know everything about an issue. However, one has a moral obligation to become informed about issues that affect him, his family, and his community. When one is not given the information that is needed, or the information is intentionally presented out of context, the average "Joe" will not use intellect to make a decision. Often, the real issue is diverted onto another topic. For example:

---

[113] Serial numbers can be put into a lead bullet by embedding RFID microchips in each one.
[114] Columbine - referring to the school shootings in Columbine High School in Littleton, Colorado.

People who are pro- "gun-control", will argue that *"You really don't need an M-16 to go duck hunting"*, and so, in their ill-informed and therefore aberrated logic, M-16s and all automatic weapons should be banned.

However, the intent of the 2nd Amendment was <u>not</u> so you and I could be free to go duck hunting (you <u>would</u> get a lot more ducks with an M-16!). The intent of the 2nd Amendment was to enable the citizens of this nation to defend themselves against their own government... but people educated in our dumbed-down society these last 40 or 50 years, were never taught their history properly.

Politicians, along with the best mind-bending psychiatrists your hard-earned tax money can buy, are experts in covertly diverting the topic from the real issue ("a well-regulated militia"[115]) onto something that is a complete *non sequituer*[116] ("you don't need an 'assault rifle' to go duck hunting").

This "phenomenon", coupled with the fact that problems seem to arise faster than they can be identified and solved, is why this country is in the horrible mess it is in today. The public has shirked its collective responsibilities, "hiring" the government (via taxes) to do what the local communities should be doing for themselves. Politicians seeking office are all too eager to propose these ludicrous "solutions" in order to mitigate the public's dissonance, and get their votes.

The Psychopolitician[117] skillfully manipulates the public's perception of reality. As an investigator, or an "average Joe", be aware that if it sounds too good to be true, it is probably a lie.

Remember that it is your own cognitive dissonance[118] that drives you to ask questions. If you are too liberal on what you accept as truthful

---

[115] Exact wording of the 2nd Amendment.

[116] *Non-sequituer* - (Latin, legal term) - "it does not follow".

[117] Psychopolitician – A politician who employs psychology. See my book *"A Synthesis of The Russian Brainwashing Manual on Psychopolitics"* on www.Net4TruthUSA.com or www.LuLu.com/Net4TruthUSA

[118] Cognitive Dissonance is the condition that arises when a person tries to hold two conflicting conclusions both true simultaneously. This is described in detail in many books on psychology, and a section of this book is devoted to this important topic. Dissonance theory is perhaps the ONLY valid observation in psychiatry.

or factual, your investigation will come to a premature dead-end, and the case will not be solved. If you allow your anger to steer you into a "witch hunt", inevitably, you'll not only fail, but you'll be snared by your own consideration. Integrity, above all, is the name of the game.

On the other hand, if you are too skeptical; i.e. you never rest in the sufficiency of evidence, you are likely to be asking questions indefinitely, and the case will persist. The balance is not an easy one to achieve, and perhaps finding what is meant by "truth", "evidence", and "facts" will help clarify where to "draw the line" in your investigations. We will do that next.

A word to the wise:

"If you stand for nothing, you'll fall for anything".

EVIDENCE, FACTS, and TRUTH

Most people think these three terms mean the same thing, and it is common to hear them used interchangeably. Part of the basic problem is the bastardization of the English-language due to the "dumbed-down" education system, and part of it is due to TV media, which inaccurately portrays our "justice system" in an inaccurate light... as practically infallible. The courts never explain any of this to a jury, and that is the reason why we have so many "made" criminals in our (U.S.) prisons – an incarceration rate that is 6 to 19 times[119] the per capita rate[120] of other Western European countries. We will give a short explanation of these terms here, in order to clarify any confusion:

EVIDENCE: Is merely *indicia* that something is abnormal, and it comes in three forms:

1: **Physical:** Often called "direct evidence". A dead body, a bullet hole, ballistics, fingerprints, DNA, a visible injury, a "blown" safe or a picked lock; a direct observation, videotape. Physical evidence cannot be denied – it is "solid matter"; it can only be explained. It cannot normally be rationalized into existence or out of existence.

2: **Testimony:** Or a complaint. Words. Testimony of any sort is inherently unreliable. People lie (cops are people – they are no exception), they also err in their observations. Witnesses can be "coached" or actually brainwashed. Their memory can be tainted by drugs or dulled by time. By itself, testimony in the absence of substantiating evidence is useless for the objective determination of facts. However, see axiom #6, 10, 18, 27, 29, 30, 42 to 47, 62, and 64 to 66, which all directly apply.

3: **Circumstantial:** (see axiom #8) Unreliable in and of itself, circumstantial evidence is not *indicia* that crime or Overt[121] has been committed, just because the situation or the circumstances would permit the crime to occur. One must be very careful not to give too much

---

[119] US Department of Justice (USDOJ) statistics.

[120] Per capita - as a ratio of the population.

[121] Overt – Dianetics / Scientology term used throughout as a pronoun – a transgression, offense, or sinful act or omission.

"weight" to this type of evidence, as it often leads to wrong conclusions and innocent people being convicted (and the actually guilty parties evading justice). What "seems to be", may actually be an investigator's own ideas and biases (based on past experience with "similar cases"), being exploited by the "drive" of one's own dissonance, motivating him or her to get a case solved.

FACTS: Are simply evidence (or *indicia*) that has been substantiated as real by direct observation, or by other means of scientific proof that validates the evidence as credible, reliable, and relevant to case being investigated.

TRUTH: Is the reality of a situation. It is what logic and reason operating upon all the relevant and available facts, determine can be agreed upon as what "must be" or "what must have happened" in a particular case. Truth is the exact consideration of a set of empirical[122] facts.

※   *"Truth is the exact consideration".*[123]
                     - Scientology axiom #38 - *Ibid*.

When "truth" is used in reference to a jury decision, it refers to the agreement or conclusion of the 16 or the 12,[124] which must be unanimous (guilty or not). What a jury (the *"finder of fact"*) <u>says</u> is true, is true regardless of whether it is <u>actually</u> true or not. Truth is essentially what we agree upon, or what can be postulated as true; truth is a conclusion that is not contested.[125]

An investigation that sets out to "prove" an investigator's foregone conclusion is, by definition, a witch-hunt (see axiom #23). A good investigator never allows his personal opinions, biases, or emotions to contaminate a case. Someone who can readily admit an error; knows he's human and <u>not</u> infallible, is not easily sidetracked, and resolves cases quickly and accurately, and therefore, finally.

---

[122] Empirical – derived from direct experience; testable; verifiable; surviving practical tests of verity.
[123] "*What Is Scientology*" - *Id* at 658 – Bridge Publications – ISBN 1-57318-122-6 see: www.bridgepub.com
[124] "16 or 12" - refers to the number of persons on a Grand Jury or Criminal Trial Jury, respectively.
[125] The matter can be uncontested for any number of reasons - including the inability to prove a negative.

One who sets out to "prove" his own ideas or conclusions may seem to succeed short-term, but because there are lies and false data in the case, the case will persist. Ultimately, it is an embarrassment and a lawsuit. Psychologists and those who subscribe to psychiatry's tenets are prone to error, since they are loathe to deal in empirical facts. Personal biases, and perceptions colored by the most aberrated "science falsely so-called",[126] have no place, where precise investigations are required.

Now that we have that covered that, we can move on....

Food for thought:

✳   #58:   *"Once one accepts a logical contradiction, one can prove anything one likes – it is the end of rational thought".* [127]

"The truth sets you free? Let's keep it real! If O.J. Simpson told the truth, he [would] *be cooking Jack Mack* [128] *with us right now".*
- "Shah" – 2-company, A-Block – Wende prison, Alden, New York, May 2003

But most importantly:

#60: *"Once you've learned to lie to yourself, lying to others becomes the natural thing to do".*
– Honor Bound Magazine,[129] Winter 2003

---

[126] "...science falsely so-called" – from 1 Timothy 6:20 KJV.
[127] The Cosmic Code - Simon & Schuster - *Id* at 158, ¶1 – ISBN 0671-24802-2
[128] Jack Mack - Jack Mackerel - a favorite fish of NY prisoners (comes in a can).
[129] Honor Bound Magazine – see: www.honorbound.com

TWO WAYS TO LIE

There are two ways of lying, as there are two ways of deceiving a customer. If a scale registers 15 ounces, you can say, "it's a pound". Your lie will remain relative to an invariable measure of the true. If the customer checks it, he can see he is being robbed, and he knows by how much you are robbing him; a truth remains as a judge between you. But if you tamper with the scale itself, it is the criterion of truth, which is denatured; there is no longer any possible control, and little by little you will forget that you're cheating. You may even bet that you will exercise all your scruples in giving exact weight, perhaps by adding a few pinches for "good measure", for the smile of the buyer and the satisfaction of your virtue. That is "pure" lying; the moment you falsified the scale of truth itself, all your virtues are at the service of evil, and are accomplices in its contagion".[130]

– Denis deRougement - "The Devil's Share"

---

[130] "The Devil's Share" - Denis DeRougement - ISBN 040-4184-316

ONE
BASIC
TRUTH CAN
BE USED AS A
FOUNDATION FOR
A MOUNTAIN OF LIES
AND IF WE DIG DOWN DEEP
ENOUGH IN THE MOUNTAIN OF
LIES AND BRING OUT THAT TRUTH
TO SEE IT ON TOP OF THE MOUNTAIN
OF LIES; THE ENTIRE MOUNTAIN OF LIES
WILL CRUMBLE UNDER THE WEIGHT OF THAT
ONE TRUTH, AND THERE IS NOTHING MORE
DEVASTATING TO A STRUCTURE OF LIES THAN THE
REVELATION OF THE TRUTH UPON WHICH THE
STRUCTURE OF LIES WAS BUILT, BECAUSE THE
SHOCK WAVES OF THE REVELATION OF THE TRUTH
REVERBERATE, AND CONTINUE TO REVERBERATE
THROUGHOUT THE EARTH FOR GENERATIONS TO
FOLLOW, AWAKENING EVEN THOSE
PEOPLE WHO HAD NO
DESIRE TO BE
AWAKENED
TO THE
TRUTH

- Delamer Duverus

OUT OF CONTEXT

At the start of the summer of 1991, two friends and I, who met years earlier at Consumer Electronics Show in Chicago, conspired to write the next best-selling science-fiction novel. Writing a book was something I had always aspired to do, and this was a subject that I could get into. I am an avid sci-fi fan, and now I had the assistance of a professor of English literature, and a self-styled expert on linguistics, with the distinction of being the first person to write the best interactive text-based video game that actually understood what was being typed. You could actually carry on an intelligent conversation with her characters. After outlining the basic plot, we started to write a sure-to-be New York Times bestseller, but because of situations that arose, we never got to finish it. The following is a few lines of text from that novel. Maybe someday, I'll get to finish it. Here is the start of it, anyway:

A King's ransom in jewels and precious stones was sold to fund this precarious mission; the journey was so dangerous, that many of the government's most astute and learned scientists and advisers considered such undertaking suicide. "Surely", they said, "the proposed mission would be one from which the ships and crew would never return". Almost everyone, who had any influence at all, attempted to dissuade the government from taking any part in (Chris's) far-fetched fantasy. "The man is obviously insane", they said, "and his claim to being an expert navigator will not bring back the ships and crew from beyond that abyss. There can be no navigation where there are no points of reference. No one has ever returned from that region, and this mission won't be any different. This man has a death wish, and he has convinced others of his lunatic fantasies. This committee respectfully recommends that funding be withdrawn".

The panel of experts knew what they were talking about. They were operating with known facts. It was true that anyone who had ever tried to journey into this uncharted region was never seen or heard from again. The mission was a quest into the unknown, that fearful place beyond which the most powerful telescopes could not see... a journey beyond what could be imagined, into the vast undiscovered territory.

It was unclear it even to the man who proposed it, what was to be gained by undertaking this enormous risk. Perhaps they would discover alien civilizations; technology, and material wealth, along with knowledge beyond their wildest dreams. Perhaps they would gain a better understanding of just what exactly lies beyond that region which had been a barrier for hundreds of years, and which had become known to ship's captains and navigators as "The Edge". To them, it was the end of the familiar, and a point of no return that no one in their right mind dared to venture into.

The region they proposed to explore was not only uncharted and unfamiliar, no one in their right minds, and in fear of their lives, ever ventured into it. Heated debates followed, but despite all of the expert's negative comments and opinions, the one person in the government who had the most influence in the decision to deny or grant the proposal, fortunately, also had the most insight. After all of the arguments had been presented, she granted permission for the three ships and their crews to venture where no man has gone before. The mission was to become one of the most noted achievements in human history. Science advanced a hundred years or more upon the crossing of the barrier, because of what they found. It was as the proposal stated it would be: a success... more so than a skeptical scientist's wildest dreams...

Quite a lead-in to what could have led into a story about the exploration of distant galaxies and discovery of alien life forms on another planet; the above dissertation is actually an adapted and reworded account of the journey of Christopher Columbus, and the discovery of the New World.

As for my claims earlier, the whole thing was a lie... that is the part that pertains to writing a sci-fi novel. I set this up purposely to get you into the mode of thinking that what was to follow had something to do with science-fiction, or a novel about space exploration.

There was nothing in the narrative that specifically mentioned outer space, planets, or extraterrestrial life. These things were all your assumptions, based on what I led you to believe with the opening statement. Since you evaluated the opening text of the story in your own mind in the context of science fiction, it was easy and natural to assume that the narration was, in fact, a sci-fi story.

In fact, this is the story of Christopher Columbus' "discovery" of the New World, proving that the Earth wasn't flat, <u>NOT</u> about three [space] ships that were going to voyage past the boundaries of the known universe.

Let's examine how I deceived you:

First of all, I "set the stage" by lying and telling you that a few friends and I started to write a sci-fi story, and that the text that followed was excerpted from that story. The truth is that I did corroborate on a short novella in 1991 along those same lines, but not <u>this</u> one. The half-truth is that in Columbus's day, a voyage such as he undertook, would have been science fiction, had he not actually accomplished what he set out to do.

The part in the narrative that states the danger of the "mission" is fact; however, the reader naturally confuses what "mission" the writer is talking about. It is easy to imagine that there would be no "point of reference" for navigation in uncharted space.

"Alien civilizations" could just as easily refer to the Native Americans of North America, as well as to people on another planet, and vice versa.

All of the other "buzzwords" in the narration such as *"abyss"*, *"funding"*, *"science"*, *"barrier"*, and the context in which they are used, all imply that this story takes place in the future, and is an undertaking sanctioned by a modern government.

The phrase *"where no man has gone before"* strikes a chord with all the fans of the original Star Trek series. In a group of people where there is just one "Trekker", the use of that exact phrase in the story may be seen as a plagiarism on my part, of the opening of each Star Trek episode. However, it convinces him that the story is science fiction (however bad or ill conceived it may be). That person's influence on the group will have them all convinced that the narrative is science fiction rather than a modern-day description of a historical event.

"Telescopes" also imply space exploration – one assumes that a telescope would be used for looking out into space.

The point of all of this is to illustrate how any one of us, a group of people, or our entire nation for that matter, can be deceived by words, and by things presented out of context. Modern politics is replete with examples of people being deceived by lies being told without the liar being specific or clear enough to be charged with perjury (Bill Clinton's testimony in the Monica Lewinsky case), or with defamation of character when things are implied, or in hundreds of courtroom testimonies. Politicians and lawyers know this all too well, and are experts in the psychology of such things. Never assume anything from what is said or written. If it is in any way nebulous or nonspecific, it probably is deception in its purest form. Paucity is always an "Orange Alert" for a lie (Axiom # 65). In this matter, many politicians have succeeded in defeating their opponents by libel and slander done with implications that are just enough to be believable, but not enough to legally constitute an actionable tort.[131] In hundreds of cases around the country, nebulously worded indictments are handed down; the details edited for fear of being caught in a lie. There is no remedy to the situation, the English language lends itself well to "covert negatives"; things that are implied and structured to be understood in the manner intended, without having to actually come out and say it.

It is not the intelligence of the reader that is questioned, but his/her own presumptions and biases which are naturally occurring, that are exploited by those who are familiar with the psychology of deception. This is the same technique used by Park Avenue marketing firms to produce deceptive ads and write scripts for political speeches. It is difficult to argue against your own conclusions, and I must admit, I have used a variation of this technique myself. With this little treatise in mind, perhaps you will see election campaigns, NEWS programs, and court testimony in a different light, and with a fresh perspective. Perhaps this time, you will <u>NOT</u> be so easily fooled.

---

[131] Actionable Tort - Grounds for a lawsuit; a lawsuit that is not frivolous.

TECHNIQUES

EAVESDROPPING: The best source of information is the unfettered spoken word of a suspect. Before you "listen in" on a conversation, you should clearly define what you wish to do with the

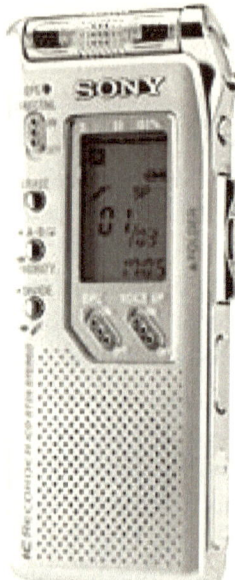

information. If the conversation is to be recorded for use in court, make certain that you thoroughly research the law on the admissibility of the evidence. This is tricky, but as a general rule, if one party of a recorded conversation is aware that it is being recorded, it is admissible as direct evidence: "probable cause" is not required. This recording is not a "wiretap". A wiretap is an electronic monitoring of a conversation where neither party is aware that it is being taped. A "tap" requires a court order, since the parties involved have a reasonable expectation of privacy. Of course, there are exceptions. Any conversation that is conducted over the public airwaves, such as over CB or Ham radio, walkie-talkie, or even a cordless phone or cell phone, is "public domain", and can be legally recorded by anyone. Digital "tape" recorders and high capacity / quick charging batteries are indispensable for such purposes.[132] The advantage to digital recordings is that they can be archived onto CD or DVD, and E-mailed to fellow investigators (if the files does not exceed your ISP's E-mail limitations).

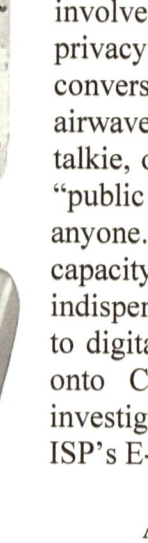

As a rule, a person "wearing a wire" or tape recording a conversation between himself and another person or persons is legal, because one party is aware of the recording.

---

[132] I personally recommend the Sony model # ICD-ST25VTP Digital Voice Recorder, which is sensitive enough to record every word spoken in a room, and in LP (mono) mode, can record 11-½ hours continuously. The recorder comes with PC (USB) interface cable and software to archive your recordings. It operates on two AAA batteries (I recommend the Radio Shack IC3 rechargeable batteries which charge in 15 minutes, and deliver 2,000 MAH – the same energy capacity as a standard "D" battery). These batteries will operate the recorder continuously for eight hours.

There are amplified listening devices such as "sound dishes" (which resemble small satellite antennas) and highly directional "shotgun" microphones, [133] which can pick up conversations at long distances over open terrain. However, because two people out in a rowboat in the middle of a lake have a reasonable expectation of privacy, someone a mile away using the "sound dish" to record their colloquy cannot enter the recording into evidence, nor refer to that conversation as a source of his information. This is not meant to be legal discourse, but as a rule, the evidence that is gained by or discovered by the use of illegal means, will (should be) dismissed as *"fruit of the poisonous tree".*[134] Police have been known to use illegal wiretaps to listen in on telephone conversations such as:

"... OK, two keys.[135] Bring the money to the McDonald's parking lot at 2 a.m. Tuesday got that?"

"... Yeah, 2 a.m. Tuesday. Come by yourself".

" OK, you be alone, too".

The cops will then "arrange" to be at McDonald's that day, "for a cup of coffee" and will "just happen to be there" by some prearranged explanation, when the deal "goes down". The fact that the "deal" going down was learned of by an illegal wiretap is never mentioned. Many of the busts that are said to be the result of "pure luck", are really the result of some sort of illegal surveillance that if discovered, would render the case against the defendant moot, because the evidence so obtained is inadmissible. If the suspect was to learn of the illegal wiretap, and that the information obtained thereby led to his arrest, the court would have to dismiss the case with prejudice.[136] However, it is doubtful that the drugs would be returned. The money, if it were not stolen, would also have to be returned, and the defendants set free.

---

[133] Shotgun microphone - a highly directional, noise-canceling unit which is very sensitive primarily in one direction, and attenuates all sounds to the sides.

[134] "Fruit of the poisonous tree" is a legal doctrine that supposes that all evidence gathered in a case is inadmissible if the premise for the collection of that evidence was false, or the allegations started with falsehoods.

[135] "Keys" - drug-dealer slang for "kilos" or "kilo" - approximately 2.2 pounds.

[136] "With prejudice" - (legal term) the case cannot be heard again (defendants cannot be re-prosecuted).

Make no mistake. In no way am I advocating the use of illegal surveillance tactics. The penalties can be quite severe, and you can be held civilly liable for invasion of privacy. There's simply much better technology and techniques to use in doing this, and by utilizing them, your case will be perfectly legal, simple, and if not simple, at least it will be fairly straightforward and irrefutable.

SURVEILLANCE: The advent of micro-miniature cameras and digital audio and video recorders has greatly enhanced the science of "snooping". An 8mm camcorder with 20-power (or better) optical zoom, and 100-power digital zoom, along with a shotgun microphone[137] are within any serious "snoop's" budget. Pictured is the Canon GL-2 camcorder that exceeds any "snoop's" needs. A serious snoop would also have infrared cameras, which can see heat images, and thus allow an investigator to look through a wall. With just the mentioned equipment, one could get video of two

people together; for example, a married man and his mistress (or his "suspected" mistress), and have a complete account of their time together. It is even possible to peer through the walls (side) of a house with the infrared camera, to see if their body heat silhouette images end up horizontal in the bedroom.

Miniature "Nanny-cams"[138] (small video cameras) monitor babysitters that are suspected of abusing children. Cameras built into wristwatches can photograph anyone without being detected; digital

cameras on medical endoscope[139] tubes can be snaked under a door, or hidden in dolls or outlet fixtures, etc.

---

[137] Shotgun microphone - a highly directional, noise-canceling unit which is very sensitive primarily in one direction, and attenuates all sounds to the sides.

[138] Nanny Cams - miniature surveillance cameras built into a (fake) book, or into a child's Teddy bear or toy. Shown is a photo of an actual camera unit next to a dime for size comparison, and a miniature camera built into a functional smoke detector.

[139] Endoscope - a medical instrument used to non-surgically (visually) examine the esophagus or colon.

Cell phone cameras are instantly available and ubiquitous. Many of these micro miniature camera units can be built into electrical outlets, faux[140] books on a bookshelf, into VHS tape cases, Teddy Bears, and hidden almost anywhere. Many of the units on the market are battery operated, and have wireless transmitter capability, so that whoever is monitoring can move around, or set up surveillance temporarily without running wires.

TRACKING: Handheld GPS[141] receivers are so small; they can be packed unobtrusively, almost anywhere. Left in "record/sample" mode, many of these devices can store location positions in five-minute (or less) intervals for weeks (or as long as the power in the batteries last). The memory of the device can then be uploaded to personal computer to get a detailed record of "whereabouts and travels", without actually having to "dog" a suspect.[142]

Professional GPS tracking devices can also send the positioning data via satellite, over the Internet to your PC, so you can watch your

subject travel around in "real-time". This is already being done to monitor "dangerous criminals", but it is a very expensive and time-intensive undertaking. All cellular phones manufactured since the year 2000 have GPS locators built in. It is almost child's play for an investigator to obtain phone records of a suspect, and "real-time" tracking whenever he or she makes or receives a call, or merely has the cell phone turned on.

If a suspect rides the NYC subway, or uses an electronic toll card, or even one of the new Chase Bank "blink" cards, his or her movements can be tracked anywhere they go. A "Metro-card" can be seized from a suspect, and his movement through the rail system traced, or traced at will (without actually seizing the card) if he used a credit card to purchase the (Metro) rail card. This is George Orwell on steroids – good in one way; bad if you would like to maintain a modicum of privacy in your life.

---

[140] *"Faux"* (French) – False.
[141] GPS - Global Positioning System - 24 orbiting Dep't of Defense Navigation Satellites.
[142] Pictured is the Magellan Systems eXplorist hand-held GPS receiver (recreational device). It has USB interface, color map overlays, and rechargeable Li-Ion battery with 14 hours continuous use.

FREEDOM OF INFORMATION ACT: (FOIA):

Every government agency, municipality, prison, institution, agency, and office (except the General Accounting Office, Central Intelligence Agency, and Homeland Security) is subject to FOIA (aka: FOIL – "Freedom of Information Laws"). You cannot request personal data about someone else (without power of attorney), nor can you request data about a pending criminal case or an ongoing police investigation. However, you can request any document or data, photo, statistic, report, or information by simply writing a letter and stating specifically what you need to know or discover.

If the documents you request are not available, it usually is best to save yourself time by adding the caveat: *"In the alternative, please provide the information I seek to have disclosed by the release of those records"*. This gives the respondent the option of just providing you with the information you seek, which will be in writing, and so just as good for most purposes.

Note that the responding agency is not required (by law) to convert the data or information you request into a form that is usable to you. For example, if the records you are looking for are archived on computer tape (or IBM punch cards), you may receive (or have to settle for) a copy of a tape or box(es) full of 80-column keypunch cards. It is then up to you to figure out how you're going to read it. The responding agency may also charge you a per-page copying fee. If you are requesting something like an unredacted copy of the Warren Commission Report, you may end up broke, and in need of a U-Haul truck. Prisons in New York State charge up to 50 cents per page for copies of prisoner records (this keeps prisoners from filing Habeas Corpus petitions, appeals of their convictions, or too many lawsuits seeking $1,000,000 because their ice cream melted).

A sample FOIL letter (which is very effective) follows:

SAMPLE FOIL LETTER

Michael J. Bitsko [143]
555 156 th. Street,
GroovyLand, USA, 55550

Gentlemen:

This is a request under the Freedom of Information Act, and Freedom of Information Law (FOIA / FOIL) Title 5 USC §552 and Title 5 USC §552(a).

Please provide the following documents and records as requested, or in the alternative, please provide the information I seek to have disclosed by the release of those records.

According to law, you have 10 (ten) business days to respond to this request. Please inform me if the retrieval of the requested information will take longer than 15 business days.

PLEASE PROVIDE THE FOLLOWING RECORDS:

<<< INSERT YOUR REQUEST HERE >>>
<<< BE AS SPECIFIC AS POSSIBLE >>>

Respectfully,

Michael J. Bitsko

---

[143] Michael Bitsko - a completely fictitious name.

Courts and police departments usually do not respond at all to FOIA / FOIL requests about an open case. However, the law clerks working in some small town or municipality may not realize that they do not have to comply, and send you what you request even though you are not legally entitled to have it. The more authoritative and professional your letter looks, the more likely you will get results. Be precise and to the point.

Any agency of a Municipality, City, State, or Federal government, or any private enterprise that does business with, or does work for ant government agency is required by law to provide you with the information you seek. The recipient of the FOIL request by law, MUST respond to you within 10 business days of receiving your letter. It is a good idea to send FOIL letters REGISTERED MAIL / RETURN RECEIPT REQUESTED along with a notarized AFFIDAVIT OF SERVICE BY MAIL.

FOIL letters in several formats (Works, Word, Word Perfect, and RTF) that you can edit and change, along with instructions and links to helpful information is available free on my web site at: www.Net4TruthUSA.com/foil.htm

GARBAGE COLLECTION: You will be surprised what you can find in a suspect's trashcan. The courts have repeatedly ruled that there is no "reasonable expectation of privacy" once something (even something that is possibly incriminating) is consigned to the "round receptacle". Be careful what you throw away (without completely destroying), and remember that you do not need a court order, a badge, or probable cause to be a garbage-picker. All you need is to be able to "look the part" of a garbage collector without arousing suspicion, or otherwise to be able to operate undetected.

COMPUTER FORENSICS: This is a science all in itself, and the subject of a separate book.[144] The knowledge of how to deal quickly and effectively with data that may be stored on a PC can mean the difference between solving a case or not. This is most crucial in "missing persons" cases, an examination of computers the victim had access to, may be crucial in the first few hours of such an investigation.

---

[144] *"Investigating The Suspect's Computer"* - David Todeschini - see: www.Net4TruthUSA.com

I have consulted with Law Enforcement in the past, and I am available on a consultation basis for selected cases. My fees are reasonable. My book *"Investigating the Suspect's Computer"*, which was formerly "For Law Enforcement Use Only", will be offered to the general public from my web site. For detailed information on this complex topic, see the BOOKSTORE on the web site at: www.Net4TruthUSA.com, or go to the forensics section of the site on: www.Net4TruthUSA.com/forensics/ for consultation details.

INTERVIEWS / INTERROGATIONS: Be aware that witnesses to a crime may not have perceived what "went down" accurately. This phenomenon is widely known in law enforcement circles. Even the victim may not appear to have "total recall" of a particularly traumatic event and drug use and psychological "counseling" will add elements to the events, which are at best subjective, and may ruin your entire investigation. If you are a detective, investigator, or police officer, keep "shrinks" and other "social sciences" quacks away from your witnesses, unless you want to completely ruin your investigation.

In particular, children are extremely malleable in this regard (see Axiom #30, 47, and 55 to 58), and are apt to tell an investigator whatever the investigator appears to want to hear. If you have a witness or a victim to interview, keep them away from psychologists, psychiatrists, social workers, and "profilers". Allow them to calm down and then use *light objective processes* [145] to get them "in present time" before you start asking questions. In addition, it would be wise and prudent to learn what ALLY COMPUTATIONS are, and how they operate,[146] particularly if you are dealing with children. A child will often tell an adult whatever the adult wants to hear in order to gain the adult's attention, friendship, or affection. Ally Computations are insidious mechanisms. When you are aware of this, and use *light objective processes*, you will find you have a more alert and objective subject to work with. These processes are covered in meticulous detail in the referenced Scientology texts.[147]

---

[145] Light Objective Processes - techniques used in Dianetics and Scientology to get a person oriented to his / her "present-time" environment.

[146] Ally Computation – an unwitting association between an event and a feeling – See: Dianetics.

[147] *"What Is Scientology"* – Bridge Publications – ISBN 1-57318-122-6 and
"The Scientology Handbook" – Bridge Publications – ISBN 87-7336-999-3 see: www.BridgePub.com

DATA MINING

Initially, especially in a complex case, you should not concern yourself too much about "making sense" of every fact or bit of data that comes to hand. This may not make sense for cases where time is an element (such as missing persons cases), where identifying a suspect could lead to recovery of a victim safe and sound. Unless a suspect is apparently involved at the outset, I believe limited (personnel) resources and energy should be concentrated on data collection. When every relevant fact is at hand, one can best evaluate the significance of the data - see axiom # 7, 8, 24, 39, 48, and 55 which all apply. In a "time critical" case such as kidnappings or child abductions, examining diaries, letters, photos (including any undeveloped film or digital images in a camera), digital computer images and E-mails), is a wise approach to seek objective information about what events immediately preceded the case being investigated. Where a life may be at stake, you can worry about "probable cause" later.[148]

Facts which "make sense" in the context therein, are called "**in**-points". Facts that contradict others, or are not seemingly relevant to other facts (i.e. not understood) are called "**out**-points". Questioning along the line of understanding these "out-points", you will ultimately be led to the data or set of facts that will impart relevance to all the other data (see axiom #41).

True "data mining" is beyond the scope of this book, but it is being used by US DOD and Homeland Security in the unlawful scrutiny of every Internet E-mail sent "in the clear", to (allegedly) ferret out possible connections to Middle East "terrorist" organizations. Data Mining is a colossal expense, and usually a waste of valuable time and resources. The results of this technique as of this writing (January 2006), has yielded only the capture of a nut-job who boasted about how he was going to cut down the Brooklyn Bridge with a hand-held blowtorch (surely, you jest!). It is my opinion that when an investigator "goes fishing" in "unknown waters", he is more likely to "catch" an old boot or car tire than a fish. The moral of the story here, is – have probable cause and a warrant before you cast your line too far.

---

[148] Law Enforcement can petition the FISA Court for warrants *ex-post-facto.*

VOICE STRESS ANALYSIS: This is not a science by any means; if one detects (or hears) "stress" in someone's voice, it only means is that the person being questioned is under stress… his shoes could be too tight, he may have to go to the bathroom (or his hemorrhoids could be acting up) for all you know.

POLYGRAPHS: Another bit of "scientific" quackery that is slightly less accurate (statistically) than tealeaf reading. Certain TV shows have given undeserved credibility to "lie detectors", which can do no such thing. If you are asked to take a polygraph test, or if you are an investigator who is thinking about giving the "results" of one any credibility at all, see the web site at: www.polygraph.com first.

BLUFFING: By using "scientific" equipment in an interrogation, an interviewer might be able to get his subject to "spill the beans", if the subject believes[149] the voice stress analyzers and / or polygraph machines "actually work" (i.e. are reliable indicators of lies). One might employ these devices (or mock-ups of such devices) "for show", as the investigator questions the subject on things which the interviewer is certain are true or false. The operator of the device can then announce (as the questioning proceeds); "he's lying", or "he's telling the truth", as the case may be. If the person you are questioning has any technical practical understanding at all, this method is best left alone. If you try it with someone who has read this book, he will know you are lying, and twist up your facts so bad that you'll be the one that ends up looking like a fool.

As often happens, the non-technical subject/suspect may become "convinced" of the "efficacy" of the machines, and he may possibly "break". If not, the investigator seamlessly moves to questioning the subject about the "out-points" of the case. The subject will either tell the truth, or (nervously) make second and tertiary postulates, which will eventually trip him up in a series of irresolvable inconsistencies or non-sequiturs.[150] If all else fails, there is always water-boarding.[151] ☺

---

[149] Or if the subject can be manipulated into believing that the "technology" is efficable.

[150] *Non-sequituer* - (Latin, legal term) - "it does not follow".

[151] Water-boarding – a form of torture similar to the "Chinese Water Torture" which reportedly yields a 'confession' in less than 30 seconds. See: www.Net4TruthUSA.com/TorturePhotos.htm

CHASING PAPER: Particularly effective is the pursuit of data committed to paper. While words and testimony can be very persuasive, a "paper trail" provides irrefutable evidence. A good trick is to obtain the paper evidence first, without the suspect's knowledge. You then ask the suspect about the information to see if he will avoid the question, or lie about the information or fact that you have already established. When you "catch" him in lie, do not let on that you know the truth. You now have a reliable indication that there is something being hidden. Axiom #1, 1c, 2, 3, 9, 21, 25, 28, 33, 36, 49 to 51, and 65 all apply here.   If the case drags on for a long period of time, and cannot be resolved, it may prove advantageous to confront one of the liars with the fact that you caught him in a lie. If the situation is then "risky enough" that he could possibly go to jail, he may "flip" on his co-conspirators, and provide you with enough evidence to cinch your case. This is a judgment call that only you can make, based on the circumstances of the case.

EXPECT TO HEAR LIES: When an Overt[152] has been committed; it is only natural that the perpetrator(s) will seek to conceal it. (See axiom # 2, 3, 12, 15, 26, 35, and 52 to 54, 62, and 65 which all apply directly). Once you expect to hear lies, <u>do not</u> automatically assume that <u>all</u> of what you hear is lies.

Your attitude should be neutral; *i.e.:*

"What I'm hearing could be a lie, and it could be the truth. I reserve my decision until I am certain that I have all the relevant data and facts, and the data fits the pieces of the puzzle nicely together as a result of the investigation".

Be careful, however, when you EXPECT to hear bullshit stories, as you may become a pathological skeptic. There is a fine line to walk here, and it becomes intuitive as time goes on, as long as you don't feed your ego by being able to "trap-off" a liar before he gets off "jump street".

🕊 🕊 🕊 🕊 🕊 🕊

---

[152] Overt – Dianetics / Scientology term used throughout as a pronoun – a transgression, offense, or sinful act or omission.

PRE-EMPTIVE TECHNIQUES

No matter if your purpose is the questioning of a suspect, a cross-examination in a courtroom, or merely to show up a liar in public, preemptive questions that lead the subject to make second postulates or additional statements which contradict provable facts, will destroy the credibility of whatever he might subsequently say.

In order to most effectively use these techniques, they must be well planned in advance, and you must possess at least one, and preferably several pieces of irrefutable factual data or bits of physical evidence that your subject does not know you have – and – that you can get him to lie about. For example: In June of 1999, a counselor at a New York prison[153] had posted a memo that misrepresented a federally funded veteran's program[154] as "equivalent" to other facility programs for "Earned Eligibility"[155] purposes. He was observed by several prisoners doing this. The prisoners, who observed the memo being posted, suspected that the program was "bogus", and covertly removed the memo, had several copies made of it, and replaced it on the bulletin board before the staff noticed that it was missing. When publicly confronted with the evidence which contradicted the points in the memo, the same counselor realized that the "jig was up", and hastily removed the memo. Several weeks later, another prisoner had sent a FOIL[156] request to the counselor for a copy of the memo, quoting it verbatim. Not knowing that copies of the memo were now in the possession of at least a dozen prisoners, the counselor responded to the FOIL request by stating in writing: *"This memo does not exist"*.

Of course, the memo *did* exist, and it could be proven; there were multiple copies of it bearing his signature in a dozen prisoner's hands! The fact that he lied on a FOIL-request, caused the suspicion that led to multiple complaints, an FBI investigation, an investigation by the Department of Veterans Affairs Inspector General,[157] an article in a

---

[153] Groveland Correctional Facility, SONYEA, NY.

[154] V.R.T.P. (Veteran's Residential Therapeutic Program).

[155] Earned Eligibility - a legal right that requires the Parole Board to prove their reasons to deny a prisoner parole, to the standard of "beyond a reasonable doubt". Earned Eligibility gives a prisoner a "liberty interest" in his release.

[156] FOIL / FOIA - Freedom of Information Laws / Act.

[157] DVA-IG investigation - case # 2001-HL-0066. See: www.Net4TruthUSA.com/PrisonerAbuse.htm

nationally distributed legal newsletter,[158] and a major chapter in another book I wrote.[159] Now, lying on a FOIL request is punishable by up to a year in prison, so the prisoners knew that the offense (Overt[160]) that was being concealed (Withhold[161]) by the denial of the existence of the memo was more serious than that.

The investigations resulted in the firing of a (male) registered nurse who had impersonated a "psychologist" supposedly "specializing in PTSD"[162] from the Canandaigua, New York VA Medical Center, who falsified the medical (psychiatric) records of a dozen veterans. The follow-up by Congressman Bernie Sanders of Vermont caused the shutdown of the V.R.T.P.[163] program. There are multiple lawsuits pending as of this writing (April 2005).

For information on this particular case – which is an excellent example of conducting an investigation under the most adverse of conditions, see my web site at:

www.Net4TruthUSA.com/PrisonerAbuse.htm and
www.Net4TruthUSA.com/TrueConfessions-01.htm

It is not unusual that investigations into corruption in the government take years; and in the interim, much damage can be done before the perpetrators are even discovered, much less taken before the bar of justice. Pre-emptive techniques can take many forms, but the object is to get the culprit to lie (preferably on paper or in front of a group of witnesses - or to a jury), and then confront him with the irrefutable evidence, or overwhelming testimony by several witnesses, that proves he's a liar. At that point, you will have that liar so twisted up in his secondary and tertiary postulates, that his testimony wouldn't be believed even if it were notarized by the Pope.

---

[158] Nov-Dec 2000 Edition of *Justicia* – ISSN# 1077-6516 – newsletter of Judicial Process Commission, Rochester, NY.

[159] See my web site at www.Net4TruthUSA for *"Wheel of Ixion – Beyond the Belly of The Beast"*.

[160] Overt – Dianetics / Scientology term used throughout as a pronoun – a transgression, offense, or sinful act or omission.

[161] Withhold - used here as a pronoun - a fact or a bit of knowledge intentionally withheld or concealed; a lie of omission.

[162] PTSD - Post-Traumatic Stress Disorder.

[163] VRTP – Veteran's Residential Therapeutic Program.

GUT FEELINGS

While a "gut feeling" is not a "technique", a good "6th sense" has been known to lead to the solution of many a perplexing case. Let's be clear about this – we're not talking about Psychics, Crystal Balls, Ouija boards, divining rods, "channeling", crystals, tealeaves, or chicken chitlins here. It is more closely related to "intuition" than anything else is, and "intuition" is not generally understood. This is my analysis for whatever it may be worth:

A. "Gut feeling" or intuition is simply cognition based upon prior experience, or knowledge that has been acquired unwittingly. One is probably not cognizant of much accumulated knowledge that has not been acquired formally, and so the investigator does not realize that he has this knowledge. This is also true for facts or circumstances in a case being investigated.

B. Since this knowledge has been acquired without the investigator's conscious attention about having absorbed it, he/she cannot articulate what a conclusion might be when *"Something ain't kosher here"*. Others, who are exposed to identical data and stimuli, may not be affected at all. However, the one investigator's dissonance is aroused, at least for the moment, and he seeks an answer (or has a "gut feeling" that something is amiss) when others do not perceive there is any question to be asked.

We think in concepts, which are packets of information that have been acquired by experience. Rationalization and logic require language; a means of articulation if only to oneself. It is a man's (male) socially trained tendency to rationalize these "gut feelings" away, because men will associate this with *"women's intuition"*. This is a mistake. It is simply (male) ego interfering with cognitive processes that we have yet to fully understand. Male and female, we all are human. There is nothing feminine about not being able to articulate a feeling, or feeling that "something isn't right", and not being able to explain it. As stated in axiom #38, if dissonance is mitigated, the "drive" to investigate further, disappears.

The question might be asked, "What do I do with a gut feeling?" The answer to that question might make a difference between solving a case or not. This is my advice:

#1 -   Do not rationalize the feeling away.

#2 -   Write down the facts you think may be contributing to your feeling.

#3 -   Write down the things you do not understand.

#4 -   Share your notes with someone else – preferably a person who has nothing to do with the case (this prevents biases from clouding what could be "obvious to the casual observer).

#5 -   Go through the list of axioms, and determine who may be lying – in other words, find any "out points" in the available data.

Once you have done such a review, you can postulate a set of circumstances into which all of the available data fits, and all of the observed situations can be explained. This postulate might not yield the truth the first time around, but the exercise will help you make sense of what doesn't make any sense, and is arousing your curiosity or causing dissonance subliminally.[164] You will be a better investigator by not so easily dismissing out-of-hand, what you can't explain or articulate.

It is very important to commit reasons for a "gut feeling" to paper. Dissonance being aroused by unknown facts easily becomes sidetracked as an investigation progresses, and other (seemingly more important) data is encountered in the course of the investigation.

🕊 🕊 🕊 🕊 🕊 🕊

---

[164] Subliminal - below one's conscious awareness.

DENIAL and RATIONALIZATION

I absolutely hate that word: "denial". To me, it has come to mean, *"You refuse to tell me what I want to hear; you won't admit that you're wrong, and I'm right"*. I'm not the only one, I'm sure, who cringes in a suppressed rage when I hear it. What is "denial" – true denial, anyway?

#52: What is commonly called "denial" is not a lie *per se '*; it is the inability to confront a painful or embarrassing truth.

#53: "Denial" or being confronted with false data that cannot be disproven causes dissonance and persistence of the case.

#54: "Denial" becomes a lie (or a "Withhold"[165]) when it seeks to conceal a crime (or Overt[166]) that is ongoing, or for which one could be punished, penalized, or prosecuted.

#64: The inability of a defendant to prove a negative, or to overcome the bias, prejudice, and / or corruption of a judge and jury, does not validate the charges against him as being true.

#65: The persistent paucity of a statement or narrative is an Orange Alert that a lie is being told.

#66: Truth is a statement that comports to reality.

A person who has committed a harmful or suppressive act will naturally wish to conceal it. This is because man's nature is basically good,[167] and he wishes to disconnect himself from the Overt (sin, offense, or crime).

"Denial" is a healthy indicator; it is *indicia* that a person's ethics are intact, and that he or she can be helped.

---

165 Withhold - used here as a pronoun - a fact or a bit of knowledge intentionally withheld or concealed; a lie of omission.

166 Overt – Dianetics / Scientology term used throughout as a pronoun – a transgression, offense, or sinful act or omission.

167 "Basically Good" – A man tries to be "right" - See: "Our True Colors" - David Todeschini.

A person who is insane by the clinical definition of not knowing right from wrong, will not believe that his obviously harmful act is wrong, and so he will not deny it, and may even proudly boast about it, or freely admit it.[168]

This assertion here is precisely the obverse of what a "shrink" will tell you. We see where the *Hick-Farmer Sigmund Freud Wannabes* have taken us;[169] so, you know that this statement is empirical fact.

If you have no objective evidence one way or another, you are in no position to make judgments (**NOTE:** information that you are not "first party" to, should be considered bullshit[170] unless proven otherwise). Aberrated people operate on both sides of objectivity; either they will adamantly deny the glaringly obvious, or affirm the patently ludicrous. Given two sets of "facts" from two different sources, we rationalize that the "truth" lies between the two extremes postulated in a case. This rationalization is an error:

"Truth is the exact consideration".[171] – (See Axiom 34, and 65)

If one fails to make this consideration, he is stupid by definition:

"Truth is a statement that comports to reality". – (Axiom # 66)

"Stupidity is the unknowingness of consideration".[172] – (Axiom # 67)

Another way to state this:

"Stupidity is the pursuit of ignorance".[173] – (Axiom # 67c)

---

[168] This condition or state of mind is the goal of all prison-based "therapeutic" programs.
[169] See my books: "Psychiatry, Mind Control, Genocide and Infanticide", "A Synthesis of the Russian Brainwashing Manual on Psychopolitics", and "The Sexual Paraphilias" on my web site at: www.Net4TruthUSA.com
[170] This "bullshit" is usually unreliable "hearsay" - there are legal exclusions to the hearsay rule, but it is best, inasmuch as it is possible, to operate on information that can be empirically and forensically verified.
[171] "What Is Scientology" – Bridge Publications – ISBN 1-57318-122-6 - Scientology axiom #38 - Ibid.
[172] "What Is Scientology" – Bridge Publications – ISBN 1-57318-122-6 - Scientology axiom #38 - Ibid.
[173] The Bible in 2 Peter 3:2 says that people "willingly are ignorant...".

If we apply reason in order to effect compromise, we end up with a false "truth"; a truth we <u>accept</u> as the truth – a "truth" which both sides of a dispute may <u>settle</u> for – but it is <u>not</u> <u>the</u> <u>truth</u>. Since the case contains lies or false data when "bargains" are struck, the case will persist (see axiom #4).

Truth has nothing to do with compromise; truth is simply the reality that everyone agrees upon. If 99% of the people in the world agree that the world is flat, and 1% agree that it is square (cube), then the "compromise" could be "the Earth is a tetrahedron",[174] or something. We see that even a majority opinion is not necessarily what normally passes as "truth".

The "exact consideration" is an analysis that takes into account all of the relevant facts, considers physical evidence, and draws conclusions that fit within the constraints of the physical possibilities, and makes sense of, or rationally explains every fact that is a known relevant factor.

I facilitated a discussion between six Vietnam veterans between 1999 and 2001, and we used the axioms in this book to propose an entirely different scenario for the JFK assassination; a scenario that nobody ever thought to propose, but one that fits all of the available forensic evidence, and does not violate the laws of physics. You will be surprised at the conclusions we came to, and wonder why nobody had ever thought of that scenario before, given that there are as many theories on the JFK murder as Carter has liver pills. See my book *"Land of Childhood's Fears"* or the sample chapter *"Vet's Rap Sessions"* on www.LuLu.com/Net4TruthUSA for the details of these (transcribed verbatim) "rap group" discussions.

There are rationalizations inherent in the process, but if you rationalize an opinion or a foregone conclusion instead of the proven facts, your investigation is a witch-hunt *sub nom.*[175] In such a case, what you are really trying to do, is validate your opinion or your conclusion with the facts of the case, instead of using the facts to arrive at an objective (truthful) conclusion. This is tantamount to stating that a crime

---

[174] Tetrahedron – a structure or item of six-fold symmetry or composition.
[175] *Sub nom* (Latin) "under another name".

or Overt[176] has been committed, then seeking to uncover evidence to support your conclusion. Unfortunately, many investigators – the police in particular - operate like this.

Investigations, which are fact-driven, are usually done faster than those that are opinion-driven. Fact-based cases are also, usually "airtight", while those cases where an investigator is trying to validate a "profile" (which is a really a set of "educated" opinions), are usually very flimsy. In the latter case, the "proof" either falls apart at the last minute, or, because lies and false data causes dissonance that motivates people to solve "mysteries", the case will eventually be overturned.

A suspect's adverse reaction to a question that may cause the investigator to conclude (or postulate) "this guy is guilty", may merely be cognitive dissonance. This reaction, which can manifest itself as fear or confusion, can easily be (and often is) mistaken by the investigator for the post offense behavior of guilt; what the law calls "*mens rea*".[177]

As a rule, a person who has committed a serious offense will exhibit marked changes in his normal behavior.[178] In order to conceal the Overt, to a certain extent, he must become withdrawn from his closest relationships. This is because he naturally is "disconnecting" from the harmful action – even though he may have planned the Overt for months! Again, this reaction is because Man is basically good, and when his actions do not agree with his ethics, he withdraws to a "safe" place. In effect, he "locks himself out" to protect his image of himself – the "me" he sees in the way he perceives that others perceive him.

A person with his ethics intact is not immune from any number of aberrations. In the course of life experiences, he can take on any number of valences,[179] which can be activated or restimulated by factors in the environment. Some behavior is literally "trauma driven", and thus involuntary. Psychiatry calls this "compulsive behavior", but psychiatry has no idea about what causes the "compulsion".

---

[176] Overt – Dianetics / Scientology term used throughout as a pronoun – a transgression, offense, or sinful act or omission.

[177] *Mens rea* - (Latin, legal term) - "a guilty mind".

[178] This is also true of a victim, especially a child, who can conceal a fact, but not his/her behavior.

[179] Valence - a false identity (persona) assumed unwittingly.

When the ethical person transgresses his ethics, inevitably, he ends up punishing himself. He does this by withdrawal or disconnection. He may repeat the offensive behavior, or harmful act to assert that his actions were "right", because he equates "right" with "good". When he repeats a harmful behavior, it is an attempt to "be good" by "being right". Conversely, when an unethical person commits an Overt, he does not punish himself. He actually believes his actions are not harmful, and therefore, he also repeats his action, only for a very different reason. A person with no ethics, or ethics which have been contaminated by the modern *"I'm OK, you're OK"* psychobabble of secular humanism,[180] is by definition, antisocial.

The dissonance that is aroused in an ethical person (i.e. one who has his "ethics in")[181] is directly proportional to his level of ethics and the severity of the offense. Therefore, it may be said that the dissonance level; i.e. the intensity of the "negative drive state" can be expressed in a mathematical formula. The dissonance level (DΔ - dissonance delta) is the potential difference between the level of ethics (Le) in an individual and the severity of the instant offense (So). The formula would be written:

$$D\Delta = (Le - So)$$

Of course, the numbers are arbitrary so I must devise a scale to show the proper relationship:

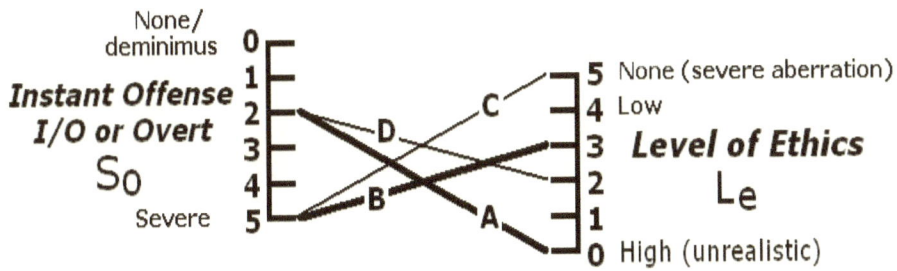

---

[180] Secular Humanism - a belief system that does not include God in the lives of human beings.
[181] Has his "ethics in"- a person who operates ethically, according to a standard of behavior.

61

DΔ = 0: This shows no dissonance or justification. You will note that a person with no ethics (who is severely aberrated) can "justify" a severe I/O (C), while a "normal" level of personal ethics can only justify low-level offenses.

DΔ > 0: a person with a very high (unrealistic) set of ethics (A) can be disturbed by a low-level Overt (DΔ = 2); a lower set of ethics (B), requires a more severe offense to raise the identical level of dissonance in a person (DΔ > 2).

It should be noted that the level of ethics has absolutely no bearing on whether or not a person commits an offense or not. That's right! The failure to recognize this fact is the primary reason for the dismal criminal recidivism rates we have in this country.[182]

What drives an ethical person to commit a serious crime? If the mere presence of "high personal standards" is not a deterrent, then what is? It is certainly not the law or the certainty of being apprehended. A high level of ethics merely means that the person will be more severely and seriously tormented by his conscience. Eventually, his dissonance is aroused, and unwittingly, he puts things into play so that he actually stops himself:

"... when a person finds himself committing too many harmful acts... he becomes his own executioner. This gives us the proof that man is basically good. When he finds himself committing too many evils, then, causatively, unconsciously or unwittingly, man puts ethics in on himself by destroying himself; and he does himself in without assistance from anybody else...

... The criminal who leaves clues behind is doing so in hopes that someone will come along to stop him from continuing to harm others. He is basically good and does not want to harm others; and in the absence of an ability to stop himself outright, he attempts to put ethics in on himself by getting [himself] thrown in prison where he will no longer be able to commit crimes". [183] (brackets, emphasis mine)

---

[182] High recidivism rates are not caused by "criminal minds", but by a phenomenon called "Asserted Rightness" – for an example, see my article: *"The Battered Spouse and the Abused Child"* available as a free download on www.Net4TruthUSA.com or www.LuLu.com/Net4TruthUSA

[183] Ron - The Humanitarian - The Road to Self-Respect - *Id* at 48 - Bridge Publications.

It stands to reason, then, that there is a mechanism or a motivator that can overwhelm a person's ethics, no matter how high his ethical standards may be. The analysis in depth is the subject of a much more voluminous *magnum opus,*[184] but suffice it to say that the etiology[185] of criminal behavior is driven by the net effect of aberrations; in particular, engrams and valences that are unwittingly acquired, and have a cumulative[186] effect over one's lifetime. This is obvious when one is familiar with Dianetics and/or Scientology. When one takes all of these factors into consideration, he is more likely to be able to properly discern an outright lie from something that may be "something else entirely".

It also stands to reason, that if a person perceives that there will be consequences for his truthful answer, as an investigator, you're definitely going to be lied to; it is a natural reaction caused by the person's own self-conviction, when confronted objectively. In order to increase the odds of being told the truth, one must be impersonal and nonjudgmental. The motive for uncovering of the truth should be to assist the person to confront his actions, and erase the aberrations that motivated them. This is what Dianetics does.

If your investigation's goal is a criminal prosecution, you have most of the concepts already defined, that will help you arrive at the truth; you only need to know what you can legally do and not do. That is beyond the scope of this book.

I have found through years of experience, that once "the law" gets involved, "truth", and anything remotely resembling truth, will literally *"fall in the street, and equity cannot enter".*[187] Keep "law" and your personal opinions, vendettas, and agendas, out of the investigation entirely. You will avoid unpleasant surprises and personal lawsuits.

If your goal is to assist someone to get at the truth for healing purposes, to resolve a dispute, mitigate a trauma, or erase an aberration, I strongly advise you to look into the technology of Dianetics, and the applied religious philosophy of Scientology.

---

[184] Magnum Opus - I have written several books on this topic. See: www.Net4TruthUSA.com
[185] Etiology - the causes of; the study of causes.
[186] Cumulative – having an effect that adds on to previous effects – becoming more bit by bit.
[187] "... *Truth has fallen in the street, and equity cannot enter".* - From Isaiah 59 KJV.

Of course, I, being a Christian, must add the caveat that salvation of one's soul ONLY comes through faith in Jesus Christ;[188] the salvation of one's sanity can be approached on the level of the technology that has been available in Dianetics since the early 1950s, and is 100% effective when properly applied. The attempt of psychology to endlessly and tediously re-hash the past traumas in one's life goes against the Biblical truth,[189] and against the axioms of Dianetics and Scientology.

Living in the past, or being compelled to continuously confront what is past; a past that cannot be changed, is one of the most intractable forms of insanity. Compulsion or suppression invites Asserted Rightness,[190] and this, my dear friend, is the core etiology of criminal recidivism, chronic drug use, and all manner of aberrant behaviors that are easily dealt with by Dianetics auditing.[191]

---

[188] *"For whosoever shall call upon the name of the Lord shall be saved".* - Romans 10:13 *KJV.*

[189] *"Therefore if any man be in Christ, he is a new creature: old things are passed away; behold, all things are become new".* - 2 Corinthians 5:17 *KJV*

[190] Asserted Rightness - a condition where the ASSERTION of "being right" takes precedence over the actual, empirical truth.

[191] Dianetics Auditing is a sacrosanct procedure of pastoral counseling that achieves remarkable results.

ETHICS and MORALITY

Every human being – and this will upset you atheists, Darwinists, psychologists, Hick-Farmer Sigmund Freud Wannabes, and Secular Humanists – is endowed _by_ _God_ at the moment of conception, with an immortal soul (or Thetan)[192] and his ethics. This is a part of conscience, which is what may essentially be called "the image and likeness of God". This is what makes Man "basically good",[193] and then he becomes aberrated over time by elements in his environment, and things that happen (or are done) to him.

Ethics is an individual thing; it is a set of internal and personal guidelines. It is not taught: _God_ bestows it. Personal ethics can be enhanced, aberrated, or even destroyed by a person's life-experiences.

Morals are codified set of rules or laws that represent the collective ethics of a community or nation of individuals. Morals are essentially an amalgam of individual ethics, and tend to favor the least ethical among the population. When morality is legislated, a nation begins a downward spiral to oblivion.

It is a fact that people with very high ethical standards, have committed serious crimes and Overts. Therefore, we see that ethics - in and of itself, is not a deterrent to out-ethics behavior.[194]

It is also a fact that legislating morality does not bring about a "moral society"; this "morality" being dependent upon the individual, whose ethics may or may not agree with the opinions of his peers or his community.

When morals or secular law is caused to deviate from the God-given scriptural mandate, there's confusion and contamination which aberrates individual ethics; there is no "moral anchor", and the individual falls prey to the collective depravity.

---

192 Thetan - Scientology's name for the human spirit that exists independently from the body.
193 "Basically good" by Man's standard. By God's standards, we are all sinners, and NONE are "good".
194 Out-ethics behavior - that behavior which goes against what a person instinctively knows is "right".

In the case of a criminal, because he continues to transgress against the collective ethics (or morality) of his community; as he is either incapable or unwilling to put ethics in on himself and continues to commit harmful acts, society acts to impose the communal ethics upon him - a thing we call "justice".

Since a man who will not put ethics in on himself is dangerous, society puts him in prison. This only aberrates the individual further, if he does not take the initiative and rehabilitate himself.[195]

The etiology of criminal behavior is beyond the scope of this book, and if statistics on recidivism rates is any proof of the efficacy of a science, methodology, or technology, the study of criminology is a waste of time. It has been said, **"prisons are criminalogenic"**;[196] that is, **they create criminals.** Perhaps you should read books written by the prisoners themselves[197] if you want a bit of helpful insight.

Basically, there would be no lies if everybody acted upon his or her own God-given ethics. There would be no lies if it weren't for fear of sanctions, censure, or embarrassment. A lie is an acknowledgment at least to oneself, that "I did something wrong" (i.e. against my own moral reasoning), and "therefore, I must conceal the Overt". [198]

"... Behold, ye have sinned against the Lord; and be sure your sin will find you out". [199]

Note: the scripture **does not say** that "Big Brother", God, or the Lord "will find you out". It is one's own sins and transgressions that act against him. Once the mechanism is known, Overts can be reconciled, and the behavior rehabilitated.

---

[195] Rehabilitate himself - any "therapeutic" methodology must be self-imposed; it is ineffective if compelled, and serves to further aberrate the individual.

[196] Criminalogenic - a process that creates criminals.

[197] A good book to start with would be "In The Belly of The Beast", by Jack Henry Abbott and Norman Mailer. A follow-up study could be done by reading my book: *"The Wheel of Ixion - Beyond The Belly Of The Beast"* See my web site at: www.Net4TruthUSA.com for availability.

[198] Overt – Dianetics / Scientology term used throughout as a pronoun – a transgression, offense, or sinful act or omission.

[199] Numbers 32: 23b *KJV*

LIES HAVE A LIFE OF THEIR OWN

※   1c.   "A lie is a second postulate designed to mask a primary postulate, statement, or condition which is permitted to remain".

We need to revisit that definition in order to see how one lie, leads to an irrational cacophony of other lies, one atop the other, like an upside down pyramid. The progression of "invented facts" is roughly geometrical; i.e. 1, 2, 4, 8, 16, 32, etc., since it usually takes two lies, or one lie and one half truth to explain to someone why the first lie (second postulate) should be believed.

The Geometrical Progression of lies told to mask Overts, crimes, sins, and other transgressions.

Subsequent Postulates

Lies

Tertiary Postulates

Half-Truths

Overt, crime, sin, or transgression

Second Postulate (original Lie)

The reason for a lie to be told to begin with is usually the avoidance of consequences for an Overt (harmful act) committed against the person or persons lied to (or lied about). See axiom #2.

Whatever the reason or motive, the immediate effect of committing an Overt (let's say the offense is cheating on your spouse), is that you must hide the fact of its commission. The immediate (natural) consequence of the Overt (or sin) is the fear of being discovered. Without any arousal of suspicion, the possibility of discovery (no matter how remote) causes the offender to withdraw from the party or parties the Overt was committed against.

67

After a bit of time, the offender gains confidence that he or she can "get away with" the offense, but the consequences are already being manifested as a loss of "connectedness" with the person or persons that the Overt[200] must be hidden from. Eventually, perhaps being persecuted a bit by conscience, in order to justify the initial offense with his or her built-in ethics;[201] to assert (to him/her self) that he or she was "right" (truth notwithstanding) to commit the initial offense, the offender repeats the offense.

We must note here, that the wrong action is repeated not because of any predisposition, predilection, or propensity toward the offending behavior *per se'*, but simply as an assertion of "rightness" against the conviction of conscience, and/or any external suppressive forces. This is the true etiology of recidivism, the ignorance of which prevents the effective rehabilitation of an offender.

After perhaps numerous repetitions of an offense, a point in time is inevitably reached, where suspicion is aroused; i.e. one tells his wife "I worked overtime at the office", and the paycheck does not support the claim. When questions are put forth regarding the discrepancy, it is time for the first of what will become many "second postulates". (See axiom #12, 21, 34, 35, 52 to 54, and 65, which all apply).

One may lie <u>again</u> (a tertiary statement) and say "The time clock was broken, and the matter will be resolved next week", to explain the "missing" overtime pay. The liar is now caught in a trap, in that he must now falsify his work records (thereby stealing from his employer), in order to create the *apparency* of a rectified "payroll mistake". [The adulterer becomes a liar, then a thief], or otherwise he must actually work overtime to get the "missing" pay, and plan his late arrival home by another tertiary postulate or statement; lying about "heavy traffic" on the highway. If the spouse waiting at home happens to have listened to the traffic report on the NEWS, and questions this lie, another, fourth statement must be made in order to convince the person being lied to, why he or she should believe you despite the inconsistencies or paucity in your "facts" (Axiom #11, 12, 21, 20 2, 26, 33, 34, and 65 - all apply).

---

[200] Overt – Dianetics / Scientology term used throughout as a pronoun – a transgression, offense, or sinful act or omission.
[201] (In other words to keep conscience at bay)

Of course, pathological liars (politicians, *et.al.*) are very good at this, and it is not such an effort to convince someone who <u>wants</u> to believe you. For example, it is natural for a wife who loves her husband, to convince herself that he is telling her the truth, no matter how implausible the story, rather than entertain a "healthy suspicion" and investigate the matter. This is because doing so might reveal the fact that her husband is being unfaithful, and/or no longer finds her attractive. (See axiom #38). Such a situation if permitted to persist will quickly destroy the intimacy between two people, after which trust collapses, and reconciliation is rare.

Therefore, we see that we can make a very good scientific case for immediate disclosure of one's Overts and faults to his or her significant other, and from refraining from the commission of harmful, "out-ethics" acts.

Lies to cover up our own faults really do have a life of their own. Once the seed of lies is planted, it is very much like the biblical "corn of wheat"; once the lie (or the second postulate) "dies", the seed guarantees an abundant harvest down the road:

"...Verily, verily I say unto you, except a corn of wheat fall into the ground and die, it abideth alone: but if it die, it bringeth forth much fruit". – John 12:24 KJV.

The fruit that arises from the seed depends on what falls into the ground. One should not expect to sow thistles, and reap rhododendrons. Avoidance of inevitable consequences, however, is not the proper motive for avoiding the commission (or repetition) of harmful acts (or sins), and this type of mindset, ever vigilant for fear of conscience or law, seeks to do one thing; it seeks to assert "rightness" in the face of truth.

Our permissive culture and the harsh sanctions of the law, is an irresolvable dichotomy of confusion that only exacerbates the problems.

A man (or a nation) with Man's law as a moral compass is doomed to failure; they are, in fact, prisoners of the letter of the law, instead of being free in the spirit of their own God-given ethics.

A society seeking to be increasingly civilized, needs to recognize that laws and prohibitions, along with the certainty of punishment is not, nor will it ever be the solution to the problems we have; in fact, statistics show that (criminal) recidivism rates are 80% or higher, nationwide. So much for the study of Criminology and "rehabilitation" programs!

There is a solution, and it is so very simple, that is buried under mountain of prohibitions, taboos, and the "*I'm OK, you're OK*" Freudian New-Age psychobabble. The solution is not to rehabilitate a man's ethics, because unless he is clinically insane, his (God-given) ethics are basically intact.

All one has to do to recover from an aberration, is to reclaim the ability to <u>*be right*</u>, instead of honing his skills of <u>*asserting he's right*</u> even when he's wrong. This cannot happen without developing the ability to confront a painful or embarrassing truth (see axiom #52 to 54). The solution, once aberration has been dealt with, is simply this:

- Do everything in love – out of genuine *agape'* or "willed affinity", no intentional offense can arise.
- Justify or rationalize nothing – if you do, you'll end up confusing lust (*eros*) with love (*agape, phileo, storge'*), and thievery with a paycheck.
- Recognize that instant gratification is like a cash advance on a credit card drawn on the *John Gotti World Bank of Karma*. If the loan is not paid immediately, it is likely that you won't be able to afford the "monthly payments" or the "late charges". It would be better to close the account.
- Follow the two great commandments – #1 -Love God above and before everyone and anything else and #2 - Love your neighbor - friend or foe - as you love yourself.

Sounds easy? Try it! It is not as easy as it sounds. The path is narrow and slippery, but "*walking in the spirit*" [202] as the Bible calls it, is much to be preferred over being a slave to the letter of the law.

---

[202] "*This I say then, Walk in the Spirit, and ye shall not fulfill the lust of the flesh*". – Galatians 5:16 *KJV*

Lies to avoid consequences are not the only type of deception that brings forth bitter fruit. Willful and malicious gossip; lies told to a person with the intent to do harm, whether you are perpetrator or victim, also grow like weeds. In our society, false witnesses, wrongful allegations, and malicious liars with nothing better to do than destroy everything in their path in order to feel self-righteous and above everyone else, is the order of the day. These poor, pathetic souls are devoid of any self-worth whatsoever, and to compensate their egos, they become self-righteous, sanctimonious, arrogant hypocrites, with whom no meaningful, truthful, or factual dialogue can be established. Truly, a malicious gossip, or someone who will hear only what he or she wants to hear, is below even pity. For these people, the only truth is their own twisted version of reality. In order not to have to come to terms with their own aberrated mentality, they will arrogantly assert their position even in the face of overwhelming data that proves they are wrong. They will assert their position, even the face of the law; and direct opposition even to physical evidence ("solid matter"), and in conflict even with the biblical *"multitude of counselors"* – Proverbs 11:14.

When one encounters such individuals, there's no mistake that the person is antisocial; what the Scientology scriptures calls a "Suppressive Person" (SP). It is best to flee from an SP's sphere of influence; in other words "disconnect" [203] oneself. If this is not possible for some reason, then have as little to do with this type of personality as possible. Suppressive Persons are inherently dangerous. What comes out of their mouth may seem to be innocuous on its face, but beware! Such may be the cobra venom of a more grandiose deception. If one keeps company with such people, or is placed within their sphere of influence, it is almost certain that one will be contaminated with, or harmed by their nefarious aberrations.

It is human nature to strive to "be good", and thus because in our own strength we are weak and fall into temptation, the next best thing to being "good", is to be "right". This is what leads inevitably to justification; i.e. *"I'm right to have a mistress because my love life at home sucks"*, or *"The boss isn't paying me what I'm worth, so it's only right that I take what is rightfully mine"*.

---

[203] Disconnect – in Scientology this means to entirely cut off any communication or interaction with a person

Apply the justification your own situation, and then examine it objectively. The best way to do this is by means of what is known in Scientology as an "Overt[204] / Withhold[205] write-up" (O/W for short). The Overt is the harmful act (instant offense, or sin); the Withhold is the lies and half-truths used to conceal it. Write it all down. Start with a synopsis or overview in a brief statement and fill-in as much detail as you can. Show it to no one, or reveal it only to a friend who will keep it in confidence. You will then see your situation more objectively.

The O/W write-up is a very simple, yet powerful tool. However, it is worse than useless if used under compulsion, or outside of a sacrosanct[206] environment. The O/W write-up should be edited over several sessions, and once you feel that enough relevant detail has been added, and you now have control or a better understanding (at least) of your situation, then the write-up should be ceremoniously destroyed.

Another axiom of Scientology #38, states:

✳   *"In order for anything to persist it must contain a lie"*.

If there is a conflict between two or more individuals, you can bet it started with a lie (or false data), and the conflict persists precisely because a lie or false data remains. If you think about this seriously, you will come to realize that apart for "solid matter", truth or reality is what we can agree upon. The conflict dissolves when the parties at odds with each other come to an agreement on the data, and both (or all) accept it as true.

In adversarial confrontations, such as in a "court of law", for example, lies and false data are flung about like oatmeal at grammar school cafeteria food fight, albeit a bit more "dignified", buried under protocol, and a thick veil of absolute judicial and prosecutorial immunity. In court, *"Truth"*, as the prophet Isaiah wrote *"is fallen in the street, and equity cannot enter"*. – Isaiah 59: 14b KJV.

---

[204] Overt – Dianetics / Scientology term used throughout as a pronoun – a transgression, offense, or sinful act or omission.

[205] Withhold - used here as a pronoun - a fact or a bit of knowledge intentionally withheld or concealed; a lie of omission.

[206] Sacrosanct - the confidentiality of attorney-client or minister/priest-penitent relationships. A visit to a psychiatrist, psychologist, social worker, or other *Hick-Farmer Sigmund Freud Wannabe* is normally NOT protected by this sacrosanct type of relationship.

So we should not be surprised that our highly-touted "criminal justice system" is an abject and dismal failure, and it is indeed, itself "criminal" in many more cases than you might imagine.

Most insidious and nefarious of all the lies, is a lie that rides piggyback on a modicum of truth. It is the cyanide-laced Kool-Aid of death; it is lethal or potentially so, because it is accepted without question – It is the original type of lie told to Eve by the Devil masquerading as a Serpent in the Garden of Eden when he told her: "... *ye shall not surely die*".[207] – Genesis 3:4b KJV. The lie slipstreaming in the wake of truth is not noticed – like a motorcycle tailgating an 18-wheeler – until it is too late.

Writing over a century ago in her book *Desire of Ages*,[208] author and former prison warden Ellen G. White, calls this type of deception "*a covert negative*". Mankind has never learned to see this type of lie for what it is. Like a virus, the covert negative cloaks itself like a *Klingon Bird-of-Prey*,[209] in a shell of truth. Once accepted and taken into the mind, the lie motivates the individual to take the wrong course of action for the right reason... or what is made to seem to be the right reason.

A *covert negative* as Ellen White so eloquently described it, is usually associated with a third party who intentionally provokes a dispute or puts enmity between others. In such cases, the lie is a half-truth designed to arouse suspicion or color the perception of one party, in order to destroy trust or confidence in another. The fuel that feeds the fire is usually a fact or a bit of circumstantial evidence that is seen (perceived) out of context, and then imagined to lend credibility to a false assumption. If you've ever seen Shakespeare's *Othello*, apply this analysis. We are well advised to temper our suspicions by committing a principal of criminal law to memory:

#8: "The danger with the use of circumstantial evidence is that of logical gaps; subjective inferential links of low probability, or insufficient degree".   *- People vs. Cleague 22 NY2d 363, 367, 292*

---

[207] Of course, Adam and Eve did die - only not right away.
[208] "Desire of Ages" - Ellen G. White - ISBN 0816-328654
[209] Klingon Bird-of-Prey - A Klingon warship on the Star Trek Sci-fi series.

Akin to the covert negative, is a selective presentation of the facts. In a courtroom, a prosecutor will always seek to suppress or withhold exculpatory evidence (this is called a "Brady / Rosario violation").[210] Although this is not a lie *per se'*, it is a lie of omission which is difficult, if not impossible to prove. In this case, the liar will use true facts presented out of context, or withheld outright, in order to have the person or persons lied to, come to erroneous conclusions about matters of fact. A good example although complex and controversial, is the Warren Commission's report on the JFK assassination. Not a single ballistics expert in his right mind would perjure himself under oath to validate the "magic bullet" nonsense. The public, traumatized and enraged, being highly emotional, and as a result of those emotions, irrational, would have believed that *aliens from Mars* did the dastardly deed, as long as the Dallas police could produce a little green man as a suspect (see axiom #38).

Lee Harvey Oswald was guilty in the public eye the moment he was arrested. Oswald being taken into custody, as a suspect, served to mitigate the collective dissonance of the nation, but the result of accepting the lies, is that the whole truth about that day will never be known. In this type of situation, the lie or half-truth need not ever come out of the liar's mouth; it is fabricated entirely in the mind of the victim – the person or people being deceived – who are guided very skillfully to draw logical and totally rational, although totally false conclusions.

Because the false data is the product of the identical cognitive processes that drive discernment, once a sufficiency of data is presented, and the person accepts his or her own erroneous conclusion as "the truth", it is almost impossible to convince that person otherwise.[211] Don't believe it? Well, try to convince the majority of Americans that Lee Harvey Oswald did <u>not</u> shoot JFK![212]

---

[210] In New York this is called "Brady / Rosario" – there is Constitutional precedent.
[211] It is impossible to argue against your own conclusions - especially if you have sufficient reason to believe.
[212] See the chapter "Vet's Rap Sessions" in my book: "Land of Childhood's Fears", or the sampler/book "Vet's Rap Sessions" on www.Net4TruthUSA.com

Others who are brainwashed by religious cults, have tragically concluded that a UFO towed by the Hale-Bopp comet, was a ticket to Heaven's Gates, purchased with purple robes, Nike™ sneakers, and a cup of cyanide laced Kool-Aid™. The tragedy of the Heaven's Gate cult, illustrates to us that there is apparently no limit to the ridiculous things people can be led to believe and accept as fact, even to the point of total suppression of the instinct or will to survive. Many other examples exist; but suffice it to say that no human being is immune to being brainwashed by people who are skilled in the "art".

In my book *"The Merchants of Chaos"*,[213] I examine a number of these methods used by psychiatrists and psychologists in order to "coach" their patients (victims) into believing what a "therapist" wants them to believe. The fact that normal, astute, and intelligent people can be manipulated is not a matter of debate, and it is not only my own unqualified opinion:

"Americans easily understand the concept of physical coercion or torture, but have a hard time accepting the idea of mental coercion or brainwashing. The American public holds an image of itself as a strong, self-reliant people, and shrinks from the notion that one of its number can be forced to conform to alien actions or beliefs, by any means other than physical coercion. A jury will acquit anyone who can prove he acted illegally because someone was pointing a gun at his head. But juries, like the public they represent, find it nearly impossible to understand that a person's actions can be controlled through a definite process of psychological mind control...

... The process is not nearly as dramatic as the term and all the mystery that surrounds it suggest. Though the results may be cataclysmic, the mechanics are subtle, and the victims often don't even know they're being manipulated. The changes are gradual, and it begins when a recruit [into a cult] *starts to <u>behave</u>, long before he starts to <u>believe</u>".*[214]

---

[213] *"Merchants of Chaos"* - by David J. Todeschini – see: www.Net4TruthUSA.com for availability.
[214] *"All God's Children"* - Carol Stoner and Joanne Parke - *Id* at 236, 238, 239 - ISBN 0-14-005055-8

This "mechanism" is no secret. It has been competently described in a number of texts, and I include this dissertation here, because no discussion of lies would be complete if the most destructive effects of the ultimate deception were not exposed.

Human beings are fallible, and all, to a greater or lesser extent are gullible. Some people are susceptible to the "love bombing" done by (religious) cults or political organizations to recruit new members, because they perceive the intentions of the "recruiter" as genuine, even though it is a deception, while others see through it:

"... I've visited spiritual communities and ashrams were people came up to me all day long saying with obnoxious sweetness: 'oh, how nice to see you; it is there any way I can serve you? You're such a beautiful being'. By the end of the day, I'm ready to pound somebody's face into the wall just to get a genuine reaction! Although the motives may be pure, a pasted-on smile and stale slogans come off as impersonal rather than personal; they tend to increase the gap between people rather than decrease it". [215]

Gullibility and infallibility are perhaps requisite in some measure as the seeds of faith and trust; indeed, it is difficult to imagine that any close an intimate bond between human beings could exist, or even begin, without some process that overlooks faults and edifies the good qualities of another personality. Similarly, it is, in my opinion, impossible to maintain "connectedness" with our fellow human beings without a reciprocal spirit of forgiveness. A delicate balance must be struck between implicit trust and healthy skepticism... between abiding faith and "spiritual discernment":

"Behold, I send you forth as sheep in the midst of wolves. Be ye therefore wise as serpents, and harmless as doves". [216]

Problems always arise as a result of willful deception; as we have seen, things quickly get out of hand.

---

[215] *"Just Another Spiritual Book"* - Bo Lozoff - *Id* at 3, 4 - ISBN 0-9614444-5-2 - Human Kindness Foundation.

[216] - Jesus Christ - Matthew 10:16 *KJV*

A single, seemingly insignificant thing can grow to unmanageable proportions; and a serious offense when lied about, can lead to capital crimes and dire consequences.

King David's moment of lustful passion with Bathsheba, led to several attempts to deceive her husband Uriah into believing that he was the cause of the pregnancy that resulted. When lies and tricks failed their intended purpose, King David sent Uriah to his death in battle, and then married his widow who gave birth to their son conceived in sin. The boy was "struck" by the Lord and died. One sin and one lie led to murder and an innocent child's death. Read the story in II Samuel, chapter 11-12, and put yourself in King David's Place. Take all of the facts and do an O/W write-up. As an exercise, draw a "tree" diagram showing all the sins and their "fruit".

When lies are used to conceal a harmful act, there's no telling where the road may lead. Quite possibly, the failure to "come clean" and make amends could cost very dearly, indeed. Often, the deception and the attempts to assert "rightness" leads to other, more serious actions. Lies not only have a life of their own; they are the only life form on earth that evolves into "higher" forms such as murder. Better it would be if a lie were never told, and better still, would be if there was never anything to lie about to start with.

Do everything in love.
In love, (*agape'*) there is no offense,
If there's no offense, there is no reason to lie.

Note: for a brief analysis on II Samuel 11-12, see my article *"Holding It Down"* in the Jan-Mar 2003 edition of *"My Brother's Keeper"* on: www.christian-ambassadors.org, or see my book *"Our True Colors"* available on my web site at: www.Net4TruthUSA.com.

<u>USING THE RAGE FACTOR</u>

A close cousin to our axiom #2, is the simple fact:

"THE TRUTH HURTS"

Using an opponent's emotions – particularly the emotion of anger amplified into rage, has to do primarily with destroying his credibility in the most humiliating and public circumstances. Using his own emotions against him requires that the lie you are about to expose is known (or was told) to the group of people that you will expose him to. It is preferable, but not entirely necessary if his deception had concealed an Overt[217] that hurt, harmed, or deceived as many individuals of that group as can be assembled together at one time.

For maximum impact, you should inform no one in the group unless it is absolutely necessary, and you should, if possible, have him affirm the lie as being the truth prior to putting it out on "Front Street".[218] You should also have a single, cutting and sarcastic remark ready to use, before making your case. Be careful not to use your anger in the investigation or in the prosecution of your case – see Axiom # 69.

A person who is outraged (that he was outsmarted) will lose control of his reasoning (he may even try to assault you), and say things that he wouldn't normally say if he were in full possession of his faculties.

Early in the fall of 2000, a prisoner working as a porter in the administration building at Groveland prison in SONYEA, New York, observed two FBI agents in a counselor's office. The prisoners knew the report was true, because their complaints, unbeknownst to the prison staff, had started a series of investigations into psychiatric fraud.[219] Upon receiving this information from a "reliable source", the prisoners decided to openly confront the counselor the following day in the "rap group":

---

[217] Overt – Dianetics / Scientology term used throughout as a pronoun – a transgression, offense, or sinful act or omission.

[218] "Front Street" - slang for exposing someone as a fake, a fraud, or a liar.

[219] Department of Veteran's Affairs Inspector General case # 2001 HL-0066, report # 01-00290-22

Prisoner: Hey, uhh, Mister "R", I heard that two FBI dudes were in your office yesterday, is that true?

Counselor: That's bullshit. Who told you that?

Prisoner: I just overheard two guys talking. You know how these things get spread around.

Counselor: Yeah, well don't pay it no mind.

The source who was the eyewitness was sitting right there, but was told to "say nothing, and don't react". The prisoner then contacted an "outside" source,[220] and she officially verified that there was indeed an FBI investigation, multiple complaints against the counselors, and put it in writing.

After the prisoner received the letter, the next time the group met, he was prepared to put the counselor "on Front Street".

Prisoner: Remember a few weeks ago, there were rumors of an FBI investigation, and I asked you about it?

Counselor: Yeah, is that rumor still going around?

Prisoner: I'm afraid so. It seems that the rumor has already gotten out of hand, you see, CCHR[221] in California knows about it.

The prisoner then held up a copy of the letter for all to see, and said, *"You can tear it up if you want to. My lawyer has the original... you see, Mr. R., I went to the doctor last week, and he told me I have rectal emphysema... must be 'cause people around here are always blowin' smoke up my ass... next time you lie, bring some maple syrup and some butter, 'cause you know I'll flip you like a pancake I-Hop's".*[222]

---

[220] The "outside source" was a staff member of the Citizen's Commission on Human Rights in California.
[221] CCHR – Citizen's Commission on Human Rights International – an advocacy group investigates and assists law enforcement investigate psychiatric abuses.
[222] IHOP's - International House of Pancakes.

Needless to say, the counselor stormed out of the room cursing like a drunken sailor, muttering threats and possibly wishing he could get his hands on some "Mad Dog" 20/20.[223] Not only did he show himself to be a liar, but also his fuming tirade demonstrated that he had something to hide[224] – why would the FBI be in his office? Either of the two possibilities; that the V.R.T.P[225] program was being investigated – or – he was "snitching" on one of the prisoners, did not sit right with the group. No one trusted him after that.

So, by approaching a situation with cold calculation, and not allowing oneself to be emotionally moved at the instant moment (not allowing your anger for the crime or Overt that was committed – Axiom #69), you can completely take your opponent off-guard, totally fluster him, and get him to make mistakes... mistakes that will show his true colors for all to see.

Once you deal with someone in this manner, he will be very wary of you from then on. He may want nothing more to do with you, and he may try to avoid answering any more of your questions. You can effectively use silence to your advantage also - see axiom #27. If he is an antagonist, or a Suppressive Personality,[226] by giving him a double dose of his own medicine, you might be able to get them off your case.

---

[223] Mad Dog 20/20 - A cheap Mogen David™ wine that street drunks and derelicts like to drink.

[224] He was also extremely upset that he had been exposed and shown to be a liar – precisely what he had accused the prisoners of in his legendary "You're in denial" assertions.

[225] V.R.T.P. – Veteran's Residential Therapeutic Program - a federally funded prison "therapy" program that kept veterans incarcerated for the purpose of NY Department of Correctional Services to receive funding to run the program. See article *"Veterans Exploited in New York Prisons at Taxpayer Expense"* in the Nov-Dec 2000 edition of *Justicia*, the newsletter of the Judicial Process Commission, 121 N. Fitzhugh Street, Rochester, NY 14614 - ISSN# 1077-6516

[226] I Highly recommend Scientology's "Handling Suppression" course. It is available at any Scientology Church, or from the Dianetics web site at: www.Dianetics.org or www.Scientology.org

JUDGMENT and CONVICTION

Many of us feel uncomfortable being placed into a situation where we can (or must) judge the actions of another person. Some of us will have as the source of their discomfort or dissonance the biblical admonition: *"Judge not, and ye shall not be judged..."* [227] and still others will fear that their decision might convict an innocent man... or free a guilty one.

Conversely, some will have such a cavalier attitude in their civic duty as jurors, that they will convict an innocent man of murder literally on the flip of a "lucky" coin (as was the case in New York in November 2000). Still others will so loathe the sin they see in themselves, that when someone else is merely accused of the Overt[228] which they themselves have committed and gotten away with, or who had an offense committed against them, the accused is automatically guilty in their eyes. In the case of the former, a person loathes others because he sees in the other, a reflection of him / her self. These people tend to vicariously punish themselves by persecuting innocent people accused of the Overt or offense that they, themselves have committed.

It is a fact that there is no such thing as impartiality in this world. Even the most unbiased among us, still has his opinions. One might ask, then, "How does an investigator keep his own biases from contaminating a case?" The answer is perhaps so simple that it evades us entirely.

We have scientific as well a scriptural proof, that man, although he can become aberrated, is basically good, and if the transgresses his own ethics, he will be self convicted and withdraw from those he has harmed. When the Overt is discovered or suspected, he must lie to conceal it (see axioms #2 and #3). The fact a lie is told (once the lie has been discovered) is strong *indicia* that the suspect is avoiding having something discovered by the question that is painful and/or embarrassing. It does not prove guilt, but it does make him the target for further investigation (see axioms # 15, 25, 27, 35 and 65).

---

[227] *"Judge not, and ye shall not be judged..."* The Holy Bible Luke 6:37
[228] Overt – Dianetics / Scientology term used throughout as a pronoun – a transgression, offense, or sinful act or omission.

The investigator must realize that those second postulates or statements in themselves prove nothing; there must be evidence to support the conclusion. By lying, it could well be that the accused is merely trying to avoid becoming a suspect, or placed in a position where accusations could lead to a situation where he/she would have to prove a negative; i.e.: having to prove his/her innocence (See Axiom #64). This is more of a common occurrence than may immediately be apparent.

It is a sad and tragic commentary that most people cannot discern a lie from truth, and to be able to do it in an objective and scientific manner. Our society and ultimately, the entire community of Man suffers as a result. In a rush to punish instead of restore; in the name of political correctness and political expediency, innocent people are persecuted while the impossible-to-catch guilty evade justice entirely. This is a violation of our Axiom # 69.

As an investigator who must investigate, it is a very difficult thing to maintain complete objectivity. The effort to remain impartial can often interfere with one's ability or willingness to rest in the sufficiency of the evidence, and the slightest bit of bias or preconceived notions about a case can cause the almost "natural" human propensity towards outright witch-hunts (Axiom # 23 and 64).

It is probably safe to say that absolutely no determination of guilt is viable in a case where no physical evidence is extant.[229] There is simply too much room for fabrications and psycho-babble to take the place of objectively verifiable facts – anyone can make an accusation, and false allegations are legion in our society for a litany of motivations and reasons.

As an objective investigator, there is no viable case in the absence of physical evidence. If an Overt[230] has in fact, been committed, there will be evidence to prove it. If any offense (vs. a crime) is in question, then there may not be any evidence other than a complaint. You should question the complaint as voraciously as you would question the suspect. Reserve your own judgment until you have all the facts.

---

[229] Extant - in existence, obviously present
[230] Overt – Dianetics / Scientology term used throughout as a pronoun – a transgression, offense, or sinful act or omission.

PROVING A NEGATIVE

Because it is impossible to prove a negative; i.e.: to prove one's innocence (Axiom #64), the United States Constitution provides for the presumption of innocence, and a codified procedure called "due process" under which a defendant must be proven guilty beyond a reasonable doubt and to moral certainty. These are lofty principles that are seldom practiced in real life, especially in the lower courts. Over half of the cases heard in this country are plea-bargained. Pleas of "guilty" have nothing to do with guilt or innocence. Pleas are a compromise on the part of a prosecutor who has a weak (or no) case, and a defendant who is engaging in risk management. All parties know that an appeal process from a lawful conviction can take anywhere from 6 to 20 years. An exoneration in such a case, for example were a man spends 18 years in prison for a crime he did not commit, when evidence surfaces to clear him, has won a hollow victory, indeed.

When an unscrupulous investigator places a suspect in a position where he must prove his innocence, the investigator runs the risk of contaminating the case beyond the ability or possibility to repair. In doing so, an innocent person may suffer, and in the process, the guilty party escapes justice. The examples are legion and are the norm rather than the exception and there are many more cases of this kind than one might imagine. The prime culprits in these situations are the elected officials who employ the aid of psychiatrists, psychologists, and criminologists (profilers) in the "proof" of the prosecution's case. These, L. Ron Hubbard (and I) have called *"The Merchants of Chaos"*.[231]

It is my advice to an honest investigator to stay well clear of their influence. While it may appear to the public that law enforcement which employs their assistance apprehend a great deal of criminals, there is not now, nor has there been an objective, scientific, and double-blind test to determine whether or not these techniques are accurate. We assume that because an investigation that is so guided ends in a conviction (or a plea), that the methods are valid. This is an unwarranted exercise in blind faith in the judicial system – assuming (again) that the court system is, as most people have falsely been led to believe "damn near infallible".

---

[231] See my web site at www.Net4TruthUSA.com or www.LuLu.com/Net4TruthUSA for availability of my forthcoming book titled *"The Merchants of Chaos"*.

The assumption that our court system is infallible is extremely dangerous, since the court system has never been objectively tested. Certainly, our court system would miserably fail the test of efficacy set forth in our Axiom # 63:

✳   63.   *"The workability of a postulate is established by the degree to which it explains existing phenomena [which is] already known; by the degree that it predicts new phenomena which when looked for, will be found to exist, and by the degree that it does not require that phenomena which do not exist in fact, be called into existence for its explanation."* [232] - Scientology Logic #19

In the interest of truth and justice – if indeed any pure form of either actually exists, an honest investigator can ill-afford to contribute contaminated data to the process. You now have the technology and the methodology to deal with liars. You must employ the utmost integrity and diligence to your investigation in order to avoid persecuting innocent people. In such as situations, there is only unspeakable tragedy, and once such things become entangled in the legal morass of the "justice" system, they are all but absolutely intractable.

Use your talents and abilities with utmost care and with no ulterior motives. You'll find that you will have greater success in the long run when you operate with the utmost personal integrity.

"Lie detectors don't detect lies. But they are pretty good at detecting engrams if you give the question just right". [233]

The following covers briefly, one of the most profound discoveries about the human mind. For a complete analysis of the many facets of what is known about what Dianetics calls "Ally Computation", you will have to study the books by L. Ron Hubbard. I cover here, only how this relates to the job of an investigator to uncover the truth.

🕊 🕊 🕊 🕊 🕊 🕊

[232] *"What Is Scientology?"* - Id at 636 - L. Ron Hubbard ISBN# 1-57318-122-6
[233] Research and Discovery Series, Vol #7 (1951) - L. Ron Hubbard - Id at 273 - ISBN# 0-88404-174-3

THE ALLY COMPUTATION

Any astute, honest investigator, who wants truth instead of fantasy, would be wise to study the phenomenon of "Ally Computation" as it is called in Dianetics. The psychiatry profession has no exact corollary for this in the DSM; the closest thing listed that comes even close is *Munchausen* syndrome.[234] Almost every adult has observed Ally Computation at one time or another. However, most fail to recognize it at all, or if it is recognized, precisely what it is, escapes them. The following is the definition given in the book *Dianetics:*

"*Ally Computation: little more than a mere* [Reactive Mind] *idiot calculation that anyone who was a friend can be kept a friend only by approximating the condition wherein the friendship was realized* [or a wherein special attention, affection, treatment, etc. was received]. *It is a computation on the basis that one can only be safe in the vicinity of certain people, and that one can only be in the vicinity of certain people by being sick, or crazy, or poor and generally disabled*".[235]

(brackets mine)

The operation of this mechanism has nothing to do with how old or young, or how intelligent or dull one happens to be. Under physical pain or emotionally traumatic or frightening conditions, anyone can fall victim to an Ally Computation quite unwittingly.

The most common example of this phenomenon is a sick child, who upon recovery, seems to be susceptible to the same (or similar) malady. Closer analysis reveals that when the child initially fell ill, his parents were not too sympathetic, because they were inconvenienced by the care the boy needed (yes, there are parents like this). Their solution was to allow the child's grandmother to care for him. Grandma here is the polar opposite of the indifferent, inconvenienced parents. The child operates on the two potentially aberrating conditions:

---

[234] Munchausen Syndrome - a mental disorder whereby a person seeks attention for him or herself, via the feigned concern for another that he or she actually harmed.
[235] Dianetics - L. Ron Hubbard - *Id* at 538 - ISBN# 0-88404-416-5 – see: www.bridgepub.com

#1 - He is in physical pain or discomfort due to the illness or injury.

#2 - He is most likely being given medication to relieve the pain or discomfort of his illness.

The child in this case, unwittingly ("subconsciously") computes that the illness he has, gets the doting and loving attention from Grandma that he did not get from his parents. Grandma is then "an ally". This is further reinforced when the child observes Grandma upbraiding[236] Mom and Dad for not taking better care of Johnny or some such admonishment. Our little Johnny, then, considers the illness "valuable", and thereafter, he may (consciously) feign the illness whenever he craves affection. In fact, the engram can actually restimulate the somatics of the illness, and/or actually bring about the illness. Depending upon the individual, the level of the original trauma and the attendant circumstances, the "feigning" (consciously deceiving) stage may not manifest itself at all, and we find a chronically ill child who would otherwise be healthy, being cared for by his "ally" grandmother.

Now, you may ask, what does all this have to do with truth versus lies? Simple. The trauma upon which a pro-survival Ally Computation is based does not necessarily have to be a physical injury or illness. A "trauma" for purposes here, can be considered to be any significant emotional upset or case of "dissonance" where a person – particularly a child that cannot assert him / herself – is trapped in a "Catch-22".

Incidentally – the Ally Computation although not recognized by that nomenclature, is precisely the thing that makes the "good cop / bad cop" routine used to interrogate suspects, work so well. In reality, this may be considered what L. Ron Hubbard called "Black Dianetics". It works so well that books have been written about it. Several *New York Times* and *Judicial Process Commission*[237] articles were written to expose this type of psychological terrorism, under which innocent suspects confessed to crimes they did not commit.

---

[236] Upbraiding – scolding or correcting.
[237] Judicial Process Commission, 121 N. Fitzhugh Street, Rochester, NY, 14614 Newsletter "Justicia"
    Call: *(585) 325-7727* Sue Porter or James Caldwell -*(585) 325-2165* Fax
    Web site: http://www.rochester.lib.ny.us/humanserv/sm0l759k.htm E-mail: judprocom@juno.com

Anyone with a Lexus Internet account can verify this by reading a case: *Peo v. Charles Grant, dkt #921-96, Rochester City Court, May 1997.* In this case, a false arrest by subordinates of author (Lt. Al Joseph, (ret.) Rochester NY Police Department) of a book titled "*We Get Confessions*" was proven, (and the case dismissed with prejudice)[238] when counsel for the defense (David Maurante, Esq.) quoted parts of the book to the Grand Jury.

Unfortunately, the Ally Computation works all too well with victims under emotional trauma, and malleable subjects such as children. A person who is questioned under stress is liable to tell you whatever you expect to hear. This is it demonstrable fact, and the subject of numerous controlled experiments, the most dramatic of which was conducted by researchers *Bruck & Ceci.*[239] They exposed this tactic of leading witnesses by conducting a controlled experiment:

An unscrupulous social worker had quite skillfully established herself as the "Ally" of a very frightened and confused three-year-old, who in order to please this Devil incarnate, followed the social worker's leading questions[240] in obvious confusion, and ended up making horrendous sexual abuse allegations against her pediatrician. Luckily for the doctor, this was a controlled experiment, and all of it was videotaped. The only ones who didn't know it was an experiment, were the child and the "social worker" (a.k.a. *Hick-Farmer-Sigmund-Freud-Wannabe*).

Victims of trauma, usually have only a partial conscious memory of a traumatic event. However, it has been proven hundreds of thousands of times that exquisite detail of a trauma is faithfully recorded in the Reactive Mind (errantly called "subconscious").

The routine questioning of anyone under emotional duress or physical pain, is therefore liable to be heavily contaminated with false data, or "dub-in", by the person being questioned, based on what he or she perceives will gain them an Ally. As I said before, this has been scientifically proven as empirical fact; the entire process can happen totally unwittingly on the part of the victim and/or the interviewer.

---

[238] Dismissed with prejudice – the case is deemed closed, and the prosecution cannot re-open the case.

[239] See: http://www.apa.org/journals/xap/xap7127.html

[240] Psychiatrists call leading questions "Hypothesized Cues".

If you do not have a personal bias in the case you're investigating, being aware of how Ally Computation works will help you not to contaminate the facts of the case unwittingly, by making yourself available as a potential Ally. If you are one of those people who routinely "coach" witnesses, then all that this book will do for you is to give a new name – Black Dianetics – to what you are already skilled at doing, and give the honest reader the technology to expose your game.

Any case that has been touched by a psychiatrist, psychologist, social worker (DSS *et.al.*) must be considered to be contaminated by false data or "dub-in", until proven otherwise.

The unraveling of a case which is contaminated by false data, is a complex affair, as in severe cases the client's perceptics[241] could actually have become aberrated. Consider the victim's dilemma: ex: a woman was robbed at gunpoint by a dark Hispanic man that she only got a brief glimpse of. Preliminary questioning while the trauma is still fresh yields no useful description, as her Analytical Mind is not fully functional at this point.

A social worker is then allowed to "calm the victim down". In their colloquy, the "DSS Lady" who has been a crime victim herself, becomes an Ally of the woman via a sympathy engram. The victim, in order to maintain the empathy relationship, allows herself to be convinced that her assailant was a black man, because in the patter between them, she learned that the assailant in the DSS worker's case was a black man. The engram compels her under penalty of loss of the Ally, to believe the false data. By the same process, all of the details may change, or in extreme cases such as the *Bruck & Ceci* experiment (cited earlier), you get total fabrications with no basis in objective fact whatsoever. Particularly germane to this discussion is:

Axiom #47:   Out of the mouths of babes or imbeciles, filtered through the thinkingness and embellishment of a psychiatrist, psychologist, therapist, social worker, or other various and sundry *Hick-Farmer Sigmund Freud Wannabes,* come the most incredible and fantastic <u>bullshit</u> <u>stories</u> ever to be conceived in the mind of man.

---

[241] Perceptics – the five senses plus the emotional and cognitive state of a person's mind – holistic perception.

Unfortunately, there are all too many "Hick-Farmer-Sigmund-Freud-Wannabes" walking around. Many of them have personal agendas and all enjoying (legal) qualified immunity that holds them harmless from civil lawsuits when their unqualified and oftentimes calculated malicious meddling *sub nom* "colors" the facts. The objective is to cause the evidence with the testimony to fit a suspect they would approve. The case in point: Vincent Jenkins of Buffalo New York, who served 18 years in prison for rape – and who was later exonerated on *Habeas Corpus*[242] petition when DNA technology that was developed during his incarceration proved his innocence.

The victim in the Jenkins case was a victim twice. Once by a man who raped her and got away (he was never caught, and the five-year statute of limitations expired while an innocent man served his time). She was victimized the second time by crooked cops who knew how to "coach" a witness, and brainwashed her into picking Mr. Jenkins out of a line-up. They did it by the process described here – not knowing its Dianetics nomenclature, but nonetheless deadly skillful with its infliction. Ally Computations can only be "cleared" with Dianetics auditing. However, it can be detected (or at least suspected) by an astute observer. Outside of an auditing procedure, an investigator can test for "dub-in", which is one of the effects arising out of "coaching" (intentional or not), by specific questions aimed at "facts" in the case that are known to be false.

If the person validates this false data, and rationalizes how it could exist (upon your suggestion that it does), she is most likely to be "dubbing in" as part of an Ally Computation (with you).

The reliability of what she may tell you – especially if the trauma is recent must be questioned. We will never know just how many travesties of justice, and how many escapes from justice have been done both unwittingly and with malice aforethought, via Ally Computations. I would venture to guess and say that it is much more common than you might think – and our discussion here, has not even mentioned another, possibly more ominous factor – the corruption that arises out of the sensationalism surrounding the national pandemic known as "Political Correctness".

---

[242] *Habeas Corpus* – (Latin, legal term) – "Bring the Body" – a proceeding to present the prisoner in court.

UNWITTING ASSUMPTIONS

Even the most experienced and honest investigators are not immune to making incorrect conclusions from otherwise good data and valid observations. When this phenomenon occurs, it is most often due to a piece of evidence that is missing or an unconscious assumption on the part of the investigator. This can easily be proven with a few simple examples:

A man left home jogging. He jogged a little ways and turned left, he jogged a little ways and turned left, then he jogged a bit more and turned left, and then he jogged back home. When he got home, he saw two masked men who were waiting for him as he arrived back home. Question: why did the man leave home jogging? Who were the two masked men? [243]

What common chemical element is represented by the letters H, I, J, K, L, M, N, O? [244]

A snail crawls slowly until he is halfway around a circle, and then he turns around and crawls halfway back. Where is the snail? [245]

If you correctly guessed (or knew) 3 out of 3, perhaps you read the examples more than once, and it would have been better for an illustration had the problem had been presented verbally (try them verbally on your friends)... but you get the point! Assumptions can swiftly take an investigation into much, much wasted time.

There are many different species of unwitting assumptions, and since I've not seen them defined anywhere; I'll take the liberty to coin some terminology for sake of a nomenclature by which to convey the concept.

---

[243] The two masked men are the catcher and the umpire.
[244] The "element" is water - represented by a play on the letters H – to – O   i.e.: H_2O
[245] The snail is ¼ of the way around the circle.

- **MUTUAL RESTIMULATION:** This condition occurs when the interviewer questioning a victim of a crime is disturbed by similar elements in both their experiences, and thereby unwittingly "leads" the person being questioned into a simile of his/her incident.

- **DATA TRANSFERENCE:** In a mutual restimulation, the case being investigated is colored with "dub-in", which is an Ally Computation that bonds the victim to the investigator by their having similar or even identical traumas.

- **THE ENEMY OF MY ENEMY:** An Ally Computation in which the investigator becomes the friend of the victim by becoming the enemy of the alleged perpetrator. This type of situation quickly escalates to absurdity and fraud.

- **WHAT MATCHES MUST BE TRUE:** Two or more witnesses are interviewed, and each has a different version of the story to tell, albeit with one or more common elements. The disparities are ignored, and the parts of the testimony that are common to most of the witnesses is held to be empirical fact. This is outright lunacy, but is upheld in court.

- **HE / SHE COULDN'T HAVE KNOWN:** A three-year-old girl questioned by police after being "coached" by a social worker about her visit to a doctor (videotaped as a prearranged controlled experiment), accurately and graphically described a violent rectal and gynecological (abusive) "examination" that never happened, along with descriptions of medical instruments that were not present in the examination room. Search for *"Bruck & Ceci"* on the Internet for a full description of this research, or log on to my web site at www.Net4TruthUSA.com for links.

- **IT'S TOO EMBARRASSING TO BE A LIE:** The victim is questioned about "intimate" matters, and presents horrific details that the investigator deems to be "embarrassing".

- **ALLY COMPUTATION:** The story can be a complete lie, or total fabrication arising from an Ally Computation. Assumptions of verity or veracity based on potential "shame", needs only one episode of Jerry Springer to invalidate the argument that what is being disclosed is true because it is embarrassing.

- **THE "CORRUPT COP" SYNDROME:** An investigator takes a statement from a victim, or a witness, and then arrests a suspect (usually without any tangible evidence or probable cause). The (illegal) interrogation then yields a "confession" (coerced and/or falsified), which is made to have sufficient common elements and just enough "denial" to make it believable. The "confession"[246] then is used to establish "probable cause" for an arrest. Of course, this is police corruption, and it happens much more often than one might suspect.

- **THE "THIRD PARTY" MECHANISM:** This works only with intent. Two people are in a dispute because a third party has secretly instigated the situation by telling lies to each of the two parties in the dispute, which either starts the dispute, or prevents the quarreling parties from communicating and thus resolving the dispute between them. Such a situation exists in all legal proceedings, were multiple "third parties" stand between the parties in the dispute. These third parties confer with each other, often manipulating the situation not with the intent to resolve the conflict, but to prolong, intensify, and exacerbate it in order to exploit it for their own advantage – the truth be damned.

Probably the most insidious mechanism ever invented that can be used (and is being used) to brainwash people, is the television set. By using this communication medium, it has been proven possible to sell the shoddiest product, and convince the general public that the most absurd nonsense is true. Moreover, even a cursory analysis of any NEWS program will reveal it to be laced with covert bias, half-truths, omitted data, and outright lies.

The human mind, when it is given true data, computes flawlessly. It has been proven that given material that causes assumptions; i.e.: the paucity of information coupled with covert implications (*a man left home jogging....*), a person will "naturally" come to the wrong conclusions.

---

[246] Which a judge will usually allow into evidence.

A good example of this is the Darwinian evolution that is taught in our schools, which has become the underpinning of practically all of the physical sciences: physics, astronomy, paleontology, etc., but especially biology. Not a single school science textbook in today's schools lacks the phrase *"millions [or billions] of years ago..."*, or *"... man has evolved..."*, or an interminable litany of other such abject nonsense. This has as its foundation, an atheistic pagan religion based on an imagined phenomenon (macro-evolution driven by natural selection, or survival of the fittest) that has never been observed to happen – not in the lab, nor in the fossil record. Darwinist evolution has a history of charlatanism and outright fraud (Piltdown man, *et al.*), which invalidates it as a science, and puts it squarely into the realm of snake-oil salesmen. National Geographic Society and their magazine – the evolutionist Bible, perpetuates this fraud and the *"...vain and profane babblings of science falsely so-called"*. [247]

The skillful deception of treating a theory (outright quackery) as science has done irreparable harm to millions, and the mindset that permits belief in such a thing, can be traced to the field of psychology. Psychology in turn, directly led to Eugenics, the "Master Race", both world wars, and the Nazi Holocaust. Darwinism led to the greatest tragedy to ever befall mankind, the mistaken belief that a child is not a human being until it is born. That in turn, led to the decision in *Roe vs. Wade*[248] and the ongoing Holocaust that has claimed upwards of 40 million innocent souls in this country alone since 1973. That death toll that makes the Nazi extermination camps at *Auschwitz*, and *Bergen-Belsen et al.*, pale in comparison![249]

All of our problems – the crime, the drugs, promiscuity, and all manner of behavioral aberrations – all of it – has its roots in the pagan Darwinist atheism that ultimately holds that all of God's creation was (really) an accident (the Big Bang), and that all life on Earth, ultimately "evolved" from a common source (dissolved rocks, a.k.a. *"primordial soup"*). This subject is covered in detail in another several of my books.[250]

---

[247] 2 Timothy 6:20 *KJV*
[248] *Roe vs. Wade*, 410 US 113, S. Ct. 705 (1973).
[249] See my book: "Psychiatry, Mind Control, Genocide, and Infanticide" on www.Net4TruthUSA.com
[250] "Entertaining Angels", "Our True Colors" and "The Book of NeoGenesis" - see my web site at: www.Net4TruthUSA.com

Suffice it to say that all we think we know about the universe and the world we live in has been contaminated by this *"science falsely so-called"*.[251] We can no longer permit this aberration to continue, even if we must collect and burn all the books that perpetuate this lie from the pit of hell. We must expunge it from our thinking before it utterly destroys our civilization, and wipes Man from the face of the earth in a volley of nuclear fireballs.

One may begin to think that I have exaggerated this latter point to absurdity. I assure the reader that this is not the case at all; for one tends to judge absurdity based upon his or her own experience, and that experience is founded upon all of the currently accepted data that one holds to be true – whether or not that data – those "facts" – have ever been tested or proven to be empirical fact.

Students in our schools are not, nor have they ever been taught the art of critical thinking. First-grade textbooks teach evolution as fact, and an eighth-grade biology test is likely to ask questions such as: *"Do you think that man is still evolving?"*

Man has **NEVER** "evolved". That is empirical fact.

Nevertheless, evolution is still taught, and questions on a test that cause a student to presume evolution had occurred (i.e.: *"... still evolving"*) are *indicia* of something more than arrogance, ignorance, or outright stupidity. This is not education – it is brainwashing, and indoctrination into a very stupid and extremely dangerous *state-funded pagan religion*.

The second most dangerous unwitting assumption that Americans have made, is that state of dissonance by which via pain of mental anguish, drives a person to accept the first "rational" explanation for something that causes the suspension of doubt; i.e.: so that one may know "the reason" for something. When TWA flight 800 crashed into Long Island sound, reporters were on the scene within minutes. They interviewed several eyewitnesses who described a trail of fire rising from the water that hit the plane, which then exploded.

---

[251] 1 Timothy 6:20 *KJV* – Paul's letter to Timothy: *"O Timothy, keep that which is committed to thy trust, avoiding profane and vain babblings, and oppositions of science falsely so called".*

Someone who has been in Vietnam, or any war of late, knew that what was being described was a SAM[252] missile. Those witness interviews were never aired again. Subsequent reports had FAA and FBI officials claiming that the plane had defective fuel sensors that shorted out, causing sparks, which ignited the fuel in the wing tanks, which (of course) fell to the ground creating a stream of fire that appeared to be a missile. Total, abject bullshit, typical of a government cover-up – and it isn't the first one. ***However, the bullshit was more comfortable to believe than the truth,*** because the truth would involve more of a cognitive effort to uncover, and "We the people" would much rather concern ourselves with the Super Bowl, or with Jerry Springer than with something that requires thinking. Sad, but also true.

There is, unbeknownst to most people, a branch of the government that is not accountable to anyone – not to Congress, nor the president, and whose funding is undiscoverable by any means – the NSA (National Security Agency) and the CIA (Central Intelligence Agency). Part of their function is "Psy-ops" (Psychological Operations). Much of their "psychobabble bullshit" is aimed at Americans, who never failed to believe any of it since the Warren Commission's report on JFK.

If man is "evolving", then "natural selection" will lead stupidity into slavery or oblivion, one.

Those who ultimately remain will be those among us who can pick fly shit out of pepper so-to-speak, or those who are skilled in the art of causing others to believe that fly shit **is** pepper, so that they unwittingly consume it without question.

We must recognize that there are insidious mechanisms at work in our own minds. There exists in our society and in the government, skilled individuals who work to exploit those mechanisms. Knowing this, it would be perhaps a bit more difficult to brainwash such a person, and certainly much more difficult to tell him or her a covert lie that will never be questioned. A man who tenaciously clings to his set-in-stone paradigms is destined to stagnate in a pool of his own stupidity.

---

[252] SAM – Surface – to – Air Missile.

To learn is to constantly question. To learn the ultimate truth, is perhaps impossible in a sea of lies, but being content in ignorance (*ignorance is bliss*)[253] is a luxury Americans can no longer afford.

What is "truth" can be considered to be what most people accept as true, but as numerous examples, history, and science reveal, "truth" is not necessarily the fact of a matter. Today's truth (*ex: the earth is flat*) is tomorrow's insanity. Ernst Haeckel's postulate in the 1800s that the (biological) cell is "*A mass of undifferentiated protoplasm*" was accepted as fact for lack of a decent (even a toy by today's standards) microscope. Today, even a five-year-old knows better. However, the "science" of Darwinian evolution that was spawned out of that lack of understanding, is still taught in our schools and universities.

All too often, professional investigators report, along with some good technology, "legal" and psychological tactics that enable them to violate all of the protections of the law and intimidate, brainwash, or manipulate the facts, in order to validate their own contrived witch-hunts. A bit of research into the matter will confirm my allegation here, and you will come away from this book with perhaps a very different methodology for mentally processing what you see and hear.

The intent of this book is not to make you a paranoid skeptic, but merely to alert you to the fact that things are not always what they appear to be. I hope that the truth will emerge from the refinement of the analytical "fire" to which you subject your perceptions and your internal biases and opinions. An astute investigator is probably best benefited by a bit of Dianetics auditing and the study of L. Ron Hubbard's investigation technology.

I sincerely hope you enjoyed this little book. If you seriously consider and study what is written here, follow the references and do your own research, there is no doubt that you will become a very astute investigator, and an expert at discerning lies from truth.

---

[253] "*For in much wisdom is much grief: and he that increaseth knowledge increaseth sorrow*".
– Ecclesiastes 1:18 KJV

INTERNET RESOURCES

www.Net4TruthUSA.com	- Author's web site.
www.LuLu.com/Net4TruthUSA	- Author's bookstore.
www.Net4TruthUSA.com/forensics/	- PC forensic consulting / data & evidence recovery.
www.RadioLiberty.com	- The News behind the News; the Story behind the Story.
www.AirAmericaRadio.com	- Air America Radio – Anti War – political commentary.
www.christian-ambassadors.org	- Christian Ambassadors Christian prison ministry.
www.alamoministries.com	- Pastor Tony Alamo - worldwide ministry.
www.polygraph.com	- The truth about "lie detectors".
www.police-test.net	- Information on how to pass a polygraph test
www.accused.com	- False allegations of child abuse.
www.VicMord.com	- Victor Mordecai – exposes Islamic Terrorism.
www.IntoTheWilderness.com	- Corruption of all types exposed.
www.WorldNetDaily.com	- Breaking News brief.
www.cchr.org	- Citizen's Commission on Human Rights.
www.criminon.org	- Criminal rehabilitation.
www.narconon.org	- Narcotics / Alcohol rehabilitation.
www.able.org	- Association for Better Living & Education.
www.scientology.org	- Church of Scientology.
www.dainetics.org	- Dianetics Foundation.
www.bridgepub.com	- Bridge Publications (Scientology/Dianetics).
www.lasttrumpetministries.com	- Christian ministry.
www.christian-ambassadors.org	- Worldwide prison ministry.
www.drdino.com	- Creation vs. Evolution - free lectures and seminars.
www.icr.org	- International Creation Research.

DEVELOPMENT CHRONOLOGY / CREDITS

This book was:

Hand-written manuscript as an ongoing project between 2001 and 2005 as a series of essays and research notes, by David John Todeschini.

Transcribed from the hand-written manuscript using voice recognition software:
Dragon Naturally Speaking v. 7.3 from Scansoft, Inc.
http://www.scansoft.com

Completely desk-top authored by David Todeschini, and published by:
http://www.LuLu.com/Net4TruthUSA/

Covers designed with Adobe Photoshop.
Text compiled into PDF format with *Adobe Acrobat Professional* v 6.0 http://www.adobe.com

OTHER TITLES BY DAVID TODESCHINI

Bookstore: www.LuLu.com/Net4TruthUSA

Land of Childhood's Fears – Faith, Friendship, and The Vietnam War
http://www.LuLu.com/content/101852   ISBN # 1-4116-2452-1 – soft cover
http://www.LuLu.com/content/210444   ISBN # 1-4116-6298-9 – hardcover

A Book of Sermons vol 1 and 2 – Sermons from WebPastor Dave's awesome web site.
http://www.LuLu.com/content/213421

A Synthesis of the Russian Brainwashing Manual on Psychopolitics
http://www.LuLu.com/content/88275.   ISBN 1-4116-1822-X

Entertaining Angels – Bible Bedtime Stories for Children
http://www.LuLu.com/content/104158

Vet's Rap Sessions - a chapter from "Land of Childhood's Fears – Faith, Friendship, and the Vietnam War" http://www.LuLu.com/content/89004

Psychiatry and Confession – a reprint of a 1948 publication of the Catholic Church w/commentary http://www.LuLu.com/content/87831.

The Sexual Paraphilias – Therapy by Hick-Farmer Sigmund Freud Wannabes
http://www.LuLu.com/content/91782

The Battered Spouse and The Abused Child http://www.LuLu.com/content/88267.

Please Don't Do This – A book for women contemplating an abortion (pro life)
http://www.LuLu.com/content/89914

The Book of NeoGenesis http://www.LuLu.com/content/89015

Psychiatry, Mind Control, Genocide and Infanticide http://www.LuLu.com/content/92111

There is always something new at Net4TruthUSA – log onto our Website often at:
www.Net4TruthUSA.com